THE SECOND COMING OF THE CHRIST

Volume 5

Michael W. Dewar

Dwelling Place Publishers

Copyright © 2023 by Michael W. Dewar
THE SECOND COMING OF THE CHRIST

ISBN: 979-8-9856973-3-9

Published by Dwelling Place Publishers
Brooklyn, New York 11236
United States of America
DPSCleansing.com

All rights reserved solely by the author. The author guarantees all contents are original and do not infringe upon the legal rights of any other person or work. No part of this book may be reproduced in any form without the permission of the author.

Unless otherwise indicated, Bible quotations are taken from The Holy Bible, New International Version(NIV). Copyright © 1973, 1978, 1984 by International Bible Society; The Holy Bible, King James Version(KJV); and The Holy Bible, New Living Translation(NLT). Copyright © 1996 by Tyndale House Publishers, Inc.

Dedication

To my granddaughter, Lauren.
May good health and the favor of God be with you always.

"Blow the trumpet in Zion, sound an alarm in my holy mountain! Let the inhabitants of the land tremble; for the day of the LORD is coming, for it is at hand..." (Joel 2:1).

CONTENTS

PREFACE..7

IRODUCTION..9
CHAPTER 1 The Realiity of the Second Coming of the Christ..13
   The Christian's Understanding of Two Advents.........................14
   The Old Testament Coming of the LORD...................................15
   The Prophet Isaiah...16
   The Prophet Ezekiel...19
   The Prophet Daniel..20
   The Prophet Joel...25
   The Prophet Zechariah...26

CHAPTER 2 The Purpose of Christ Returning to Earth............29
   To Fulfill Promises Made..32
   To Fulfill Prophecy (OT)..35
   As the Believers' Hope Realized..35
   To Put Down All Oppositions..38
   To Judge the Nations...40

CHAPTER 3 When Will Christ Return?....................................41
   Signs of Christ's Return..43

v

The Day and Hour of Christ's Return..46
When the Gospel is Preached to All Nations........................49
The Day of the LORD vs the Day of Christ..........................52

CHAPTER 4 How Will Christ Return?..................................57
Christ Returns Visibly...57
Christ Returns Publicly and Noisily..58
Christ Returns in Power and Glory..59
Christ Returns Suddenly and Dramatically...........................61
Christ Returns with Company..64

CHAPTER 5 How Will Christ Be Received Upon His Return?...71
A Hostile Reception..72
A Colossal Military Miscalculation..73
The Final War..75

CHAPTER 6 Your Attitude Toward the Coming of the Christ..........81
The Christian Audience..82
The Seekers' Audience...87
The Audience of Unbelievers..89

End Notes...93

About the Author...95

Other Books by this Author...97

PREFACE

The second coming of the Christ to earth is the only hope for humankind and the Planet. We have amassed a nuclear arsenal powerful enough to destroy ourselves and the Planet many times over. We have not done so yet, because the Almighty Himself has a purpose for humans and the Planet that no created being can abort. God's purpose will always prevail.

I am confident, therefore, that earth and the human family will not end in a catastrophic, nuclear fireball. The earth will remain here until God's plan is fully realized. God has restrained us from self-destruction thus far and will continue to do so for His own, praise, glory, and purpose.

One purpose is that Christ will reign over the kingdom of God on the earth, sitting on the throne of King David. God has spoken and His word must come to pass (Prov.19: 21; Isa.55:10-11).

The Lord Jesus Christ promised to return to reign over the earth, and the earth will be here for the actualization of that promise. Yes, there will be wars and rumors of war, diseases, pestilence, and natural disasters of various kinds. But the end is not determined by these things or by the doings any world leader but by God Himself (Matt.24:6-8).

The signs that we are now seeing worldwide, strongly warn that the return of the Christ is near at hand. But even nearer is the exodus of the of the people of God in the event called, *The Rapture,* an event that can happen at any time (see Volume 1).

My purpose for writing is to encourage the people of God to remain faithful, ready, and watchful as the wait for that special trumpet call for that exodus or departure from earth to heaven.

A second reason for writing is to create easy to understand Bible-study tools to aid believers in their preparedness for that imminent departure. I also want to prod unbelievers and seekers to make up their minds and accept the eternal salvation provided in the Lord Jesus Christ while the door of opportunity is still opened (John 3:16). They are running out of time.

I want to thank the members of the New York Congregational Baptist Church (NYCBC) and others for their continued support of me in the ministry of the gospel. May these written tools serve for your edification and blessing.

INTRODUCTION

The Second Coming of Jesus Christ to the earth is a simple straightforward teaching of Scripture, Christ is coming back to earth. The controversy lies in where to place what I call, *Related Events to the Second Coming of the Christ.* The different faith traditions do not all agree on how these events will happen. This 10-volume series is an attempt to place them in their rightful order.

While the Word of God provides much information on the time and place of the major events, it does not provide enough clarity on others to be dogmatically conclusive about them. The Bible is silent as to how some details will play out.

Yet, the Word of God is the ultimate guide in the proper placement of such events. But the proper method of biblical interpretation must also be applied. As stated in volume 1, this series, primarily use the literal method because it is the most accurate and reliable. Where the text shows that employing a literal approach is ridiculous and defies basic common sense, then it is time to use a different method, allegorical or spiritualization or otherwise. For example, God said to Moses, the land that I am giving to the Israelite is a land "flowing with milk and honey."

While it is not impossible for milk and honey to be plentiful in at a place, the context and basic common sense tells us milk and honey is a figurative expression, meaning the land is not barren, but fruitful, productive, not only good for farming and cattle raring, but good to live, prosper, and raise a family.

Or when Jesus says, I am the door, He does not mean wood or metal such as we see on a building, but He provides access or entrance or opportunity from one state of existence to another (John 10:7-10; 14:6). As a rule, when the Scripture speaks metaphorically, allegorically, or proverbially, the context most often tells what is meant. For example, the vineyard of Isaiah 5 is Israel as well as the valley of dry bones in Ezekiel 37. How do we know? The context tells us. Daniel, Revelation, and most of the parables of the Gospels provide the meaning in the immediate context. The parables tell us what kingdom of heaven is like.

Scripture leaves little or no room to put your own ideas in God's mouth. The literal method is the most accurate method of scriptural interpretation. The reader must also approach the text prayerfully and under the guidance of the blessed Holy Spirit.

This book is intended to bring clarity to the subject of the second coming of the Christ for everyday believers and seekers of the faith who want to be truly ready for the coming of the Lord. In Volume 1, Christ calls for the righteous from the atmospheric heaven without coming to earth (1Thess.4:16-18). The righteous dead are resurrected, and the righteous living are caught up together and taken to heaven (1Cor. 15:51-58).

INTRODUCTION

While the righteous are in heaven at the various events prepared for them (Volume 2), the seven years of *Great Tribulation* is raging on the earth; the wrath of the Lamb, the judgment of God is poured out upon unbelievers and the resources that make life comfortable (Volume 3). Satan through the twin beasts, the antichrist and the false prophet, lead world government during the tribulation upheavals (Rev.13:1-18).

Life will be most difficult on the earth, especially for those who wish to refuse the mark of the beast and serve Christ. Satan will not allow any person to defy his authority to serve Jesus Christ without impunity. Satan's human agents will take the lives of those who defy him. Government atrocities against people will make Hitler's Germany and Isis beheadings seem tame.

Millions will find salvation by defying Satan and refuse the mark of the beast, even though they will be slaughtered. They are called tribulation saints. As the seven years of *Great Tribulation* counts down, Jesus returns to earth in the clouds of glory with an army of saints and angels. This is the Second Coming of the Christ to earth that this volume is focused on.

The path this series take is that Jesus will first call for His Church (the righteous ones) before the seven years of *Great Tribulation* begins officially. Again, the *Great Tribulation* is the judgment of God being poured out upon unbelieving humankind and upon the resources of earth that make life comfortable for them. God's aim is not to destroy humans, but to drive them to change lives or repentance. Some will repent and receive salvation. But others will not; they will curse God instead!

The time of the Great Tribulation is referred in Scriptures by several names, including *the time of Jacob's Trouble*, and the time of wrath. The book of Revelation clearly shows that the series of judgment administered as the seven-seal scroll is broken are conducted by Jesus Christ (Rev.5-6). The Church is the Bride of Christ and He promised to save His people from the wrath to come (1Thess.5:9-11). The overwhelming majority of Christian scholars believe that Jesus will call for His Church before the fire of the seven years of *Great Tribulation* begins; it is the time of the wrath of the Lamb (see Volume 1 *The Rapture*).

However, there are few faith traditions that vigorously maintain that the Church of Jesus Christ will go through the *Great Tribulation*. Some among this persuasion greatly distort the Word of God, bending it to fit into the theological hoop of their faith tradition, while loudly denouncing other perspectives. For these reasons, among others, this series identify the main related events to the Second Coming of the Christ and arranged them sequentially as the scripture says they will unfold. We do this without being unkind to those who disagree and believe otherwise.

There are events, however, that the Bible is either silent on or gives too little information about, for anyone to speak with dogmatic certainty. If our opinion is given on these, we make it clear that it is our opinion, not pretend it is definitively Bible.

No group knows all the details of future events to speak with dogmatic certainty on every detail. But with the help of the blessed Holy Spirit and good scholarship, we try to give you what the Word of God teaches in this 10-volume series. They are written for the everyday believer who don't have time for endless wrangling with theological jargons. May you be edified and blessed as you diligently read this series of books.

CHAPTER 1
THE REALITY OF THE SECOND COMING OF THE CHRIST

For a long time, Christians have been saying, the Lord is coming soon, and He is not here yet. It appears as if the Christ is taking a mighty long time to return. This perception causes some skeptics and scoffers to deny the reality of His coming and classify it as sheer fiction. But the critics have overlooked two things: 1) a short human life span causes time to seem longer that it really is, and 2) Jesus did not give us a specific date for His return.

With regards to short human life span, the Bible tells us a thousand years is as one day to God (2 Peter 3:1-10). Therefore, the two thousand years stretch from the ascension of the Christ to now are just two days to God. Second, the Church has an assignment to bring the gospel to all nations before the end comes, for that reason, among others, the Lord did not set a known date for His return. But He tells us to be ready and watching because it could happen anytime unannounced. Once the gospel is satisfactorily preached to all nations, the end of the age will be upon us. We now know that the rapture will take place first.

The skeptics deny the reality of the Lord's return, in their attempt to make Christ a liar. But Jesus Christ is truth personified; He does not have the character of a liar(John 14:6). Lying is an attribute of Satan, not the Christ (John 8:44). The skeptics claim that the world, as we know it, will continue *ad infinitum*. This position is one of Satan's big lies to keep Christians off their guard of watchfulness and give a false sense of security to unbelievers.

The Christians' Understanding of Two Advents

This chapter shows that the reality of the coming of the Lord at the near end of the age is taught in both Old and New Testament Scriptures. But the Old Testament (OT) does not directly speak of a *first coming* and a *second coming of the Christ* separately. It speaks of the *coming of the Lord* or *the day of the Lord* or *that day*. Why?

The OT prophets did not see the Church age that would divide the fulfilment of prophetic events into a first and a second coming of the Messiah, so they just speak of the coming of the Lord or of the day of the Lord or that day as if all events would happen all at once. God gave them the revelation they needed to know.

But when Christians look at OT prophecies, they observe that some events are applicable to the *first coming of the Christ*, while others refer to *His second coming*. For example, we know Jesus has already been born of a Virgin in Bethlehem of Judah as prophesied by Isaiah and Micah (Isa.7: 14-16; Micah 5:2-3).

We look at the upbringing of Jesus, His sacrificial death on the cross, His burial and resurrection, and we know Isaiah 53 could not be talking about anyone else but Jesus of Nazareth, and these events have been fulfilled in His first advent. Christians know Jesus is the Messiah, God incarnate, because what the prophets wrote fit the life and person of Jesus of Nazareth perfectly.

Furthermore, Jesus verbally confirmed His messiahship and promised He will come again to reign. The OT prophets did not see the gap between His first and second coming, so they thought of one coming, the coming of the Lord, or the Day of the Lord.

Christians are like a man standing at a crossroads with the benefit of seeing in both directions, the past and the future. Old Testament prophets did not have that advantage.

Christians can see the first advent of the Christ clearly because it is history; it has already happened. We can also see the future second coming of the Christ because Jesus promised He will return, and the New Testament (NT) speaks extensively about it. Yes, we are slightly disadvantaged because we don't know all the details of the second coming; yet we know enough to keep us working and waiting with great hope and expectation (Titus 2:11).

THE OLD TESTAMENT PROPHETS AND THE COMING OF THE LORD

The OT prophets like Isaiah, Ezekiel, Daniel, Joel, and Zachariah illustrate for us how they and their fellow prophets saw the coming of the Lord and prophesied about it. Yet, they did not know they were prophesying about a first and or second coming of the Messiah.

The Prophet Isaiah

Isaiah prophesied 700 years before the birth of Jesus Christ. He spoke generously about the coming of the Messiah. Some of those prophesies are exclusively about the Messiah's first coming, others exclusively about His second coming, and there are those that speak of both first and second coming as one event. The following speaks of both coming as one prophecy:

> Nevertheless, there will be no more gloom for those who were in distress. In the past he humbled the land of Zebulun and the land of Naphtali, but in the future he will honor Galilee of the nations, by the Way of the Sea, beyond Jordan. The people who walked in darkness have seen a great light; those who dwell in the land of deep darkness, on them has light shined....
>
> For unto us a child is born, to us a son is given, and the government will be on his shoulders. And he will be called Wonderful Counselor, Mighty God, Everlasting Father, Prince of Peace. Of the greatness of his government and peace there will be no end. He will reign on David's throne and over his kingdom, establishing and upholding it with justice and righteousness forever. The zeal of the LORD Almighty will accomplish this. (Isaiah 9:1-7)

The preceding verses from Isaiah are widely used in churches at Christmas time in relation to the birth of Jesus Christ, because

Christian scholars see their fulfillment in the first advent of the Christ; not only His birth, but His ministry that was based in the seaside town of Capernaum in Galilee.

When Israel settled in Canaan, this stretch of land was given to the tribes of Zebulun and Naphtali. But because of their sins, they came under Assyrian servitude (2 King 15:29). But the Messiah came and gave hope to these depressed people of God who dwell in spiritual darkness. The Messiah pitched His tent among a once hopeless and despised people by making Capernaum His ministry base (Luke 4:16-31; John 2:11-12).

He was the great light to these people who sat in darkness, in the land of the shadow of death. Jesus moved His ministry from Nazareth where he was rejected by His hometown folks and relocated to Capernaum in Galilee—this was not coincidental. Saint Matthew sees the move to Capernaum as a fulfillment of Isaiah's prophecy (Matt. 4:12-16).

But look again at the Isaiah's passage, especially verses 6-7, you will observe that these are not all fulfilled in the first advent of the Christ. During His first coming, Jesus of Nazareth, did not sit on the throne of David and rule over Israel or any nation. He did not have the responsibility of government on His shoulders, but when He comes again all this will be realized. Isaiah himself who gave the prophecy related it to the coming of the Lord but did not see a first coming and a second coming. He did not see the Church age splitting his prophecy into two fulfillments.

Furthermore, the term *Prince of Peace* could also be translated King of Peace (Gen.14:18-20). The terms *Mighty God, Everlasting Father* suggest that the Messiah would be divine. But *first century Judaism* did not understand Isaiah's prophecy to mean the Messiah would be God incarnate, but Christians did. To this day, Judaism has not and will not accept that application of Isaiah's prophecy to the Messiah. But when Jesus Christ returns, they will accept Him because there will no alternative explanation. To reject Him then is to be permanently lost; that will be their final chance.

Again, Isaiah speaks of the coming of the LORD, not as a *child born* or as a suffering servant but as a mighty warrior to take vengeance upon His enemies as depicted in the following prophecy (Isaiah 63:1-6):

> Who is this coming from Edom, from Bozrah, with garments stained crimson? Who is this robed in splendor, striding forward in the greatness of his strength? " It is I, proclaiming victory, mighty to save."
> Why are your garments red, like those of one treading the winepress?
> "I have trodden the winepress alone; from the nations no one was with me. I trampled them in my anger and trod them down in my wrath; their blood spattered my garments, and I stained all my clothing.
> It was for me the day of vengeance; the year for me to redeem had come. I looked and there was no one to help, I was appalled that no one gave support; so my own arm achieved salvation for me, and my own wrath sustained me. I trampled the nations in my anger; in my wrath I made them drunk and poured their blood on the ground." (Isaiah 63:1-6)

In the preceding prophecy, Isaiah looks pass the first advent of the Christ and the Church age to what we now call, the second coming of the Christ in judgment and wrath. But the prophet does not know that—he only knows of the *coming of the Lord* to execute justice and judgment; that's what messiahs do. To Christians, this is the Messiah's second advent, and his bloody garments have to do with the fury of war, namely Armageddon. In that war, Christ triumphs over His enemies as one crushing grapes with his bare feet to make wine in ancient times; that explains his red garments.

Isaiah does not only see the coming of the Lord in war but as the champion of peace, one who brings harmony to the whole earth after the justice of war, even the animal kingdom will live in peace. "The wolf shall dwell with the lambs, and the leopard shall lie down with the young goats, and the calf and the lion and the fattened calf together; and a little child shall lead them" (Isa.11:6-7 ESV). The viciousness, the hostility is gone from these animals.

These preceding verses about the animals are referring to the time of the millennium, the thousand-year reign of Christ over the earth (Rev.20:1-5). But other verses in the Isaiah passage refer to the first advent of the Christ. Unlike the Christians, the OT prophets did not see or understand that the Messiah would come twice; they saw one and labeled it *the coming of the Lord or the Day of the Lord or that Day* (i.e., the day of judgment).

The Prophet Ezekiel

Bible scholars believe that Ezekiel 37 has to do with the restoration of Israel to its homeland (vv.1-14) and the end-time reunification of its two kingdoms (vv.15-28). The former has happened and is happening in the Church age with the rebirth of the nation in 1948. The latter is not likely to happen until the return of the Messiah, Jesus Christ.

Ezekiel 38-39 speaks of certain gentile nations that will besiege Israel in these latter days to annihilate its people. But Jesus Christ, the Messiah, will return to rescue Israel before the enemy's diabolical plan is realized. Instead, Israel's enemies will contend with the armies of heaven in the Armageddon war.

This war will liberate Israel from a coalition of gentile nations, led by the Antichrist and bent on Israel's destruction. It will be the mother of all wars, the war that ends all wars with a smashing defeat for Israel's enemies. With Christ's victory in this the war, the *Great Tribulation* will be officially ended.

Ezekiel 40 speaks of the millennial Kingdom of the Messiah and Israel's role in that kingdom. This is established after Armageddon, so the events of all three chapters (38-40) take place in the context of the second advent of the Christ. This is crystal clear to Christians, but it was not as clear to Ezekiel or those using the Hebrew Bible up to the crucifixion of Jesus. Jesus and the Blessed Holy Spirit bring clarity to the Hebrew Scriptures.

The Prophet Daniel

The book of Daniel is most dramatic and picturesque in speaking about the kingdoms of this world and the coming of the future or eschatological kingdom of God. Like the apostle John who gives us the book of Revelation, Daniel's information is conveyed in visions and the apostle John picks up where Daniel left off.

Daniel speaks of the coming kingdom of God which embraces both the first and second comings of the Messiah, but like the other prophets he did not see the Church age to make a distinction between a first and a second comings. He just speak of the coming kingdom of God. When Christians analyze the contents of Daniel's prophecies, we can see events applicable to the first coming of the Messiah and events that will take place at His second coming.

First, Daniel speaks of God setting up a kingdom that would crush to pieces the kingdoms of this world and displace them (Dan.2:44). He said this in the context of interpreting the dream of Nebuchadnezzar king of Babylon.

The king dreamed of a colossal image with head of gold, breast, and arms of silver, middle and thighs of bronze, legs of iron, and feet partly iron and partly clay. Daniel interpreted the dream to symbolize four succeeding world powers from Babylon to Rome. Then a stone rolls down from a mountain, not by human's doing; it struck the image and broke it to pieces, and the wind blew away the pieces leaving no trace of them. The stone grew to fill the whole world (vv.31-43).

According to Daniel, the stone represents the Kingdom of God that will strike the kingdoms of earth and bring an end to them (vv.44-45). This interpretation is not applicable to the first coming of the Christ, because Jesus Christ did not violently overthrow any earthly kingdom at that time. He refused to lead a revolt against Rome; He informed the Roman governor, "My kingdom is not of this world…"(John 18:33-36). That was enough for the governor to declare Jesus, innocent (v.38,19:4).

Daniel's interpretation did not see the first coming of the Christ, nor the Church age, he saw what Christians call, the second coming of the Christ. At that time Christ will come in judgment and justice to crush and end the kingdoms of this world in the war that ends all wars, Armageddon. Handel in the Messiah exclaimed, "the kingdoms of this world have become the Kingdom of our God and of His Christ and He shall reign fore and ever."

Second, Daniel himself had a vision of four beasts: 1) like a lion with eagle's wings (i.e., the Babylonian empire), 2) like a bear (i.e., Medo-Persian Empire), 3) like a leopard but with four wings (the Grecian Empire under Alexander the Great), and 4) a great and terrible beast with 10 horns, plus a little horn (i.e., the Roman Empire). The little horn speaks of the revived Roman Empire under the antichrist at the beginning of the Great Tribulation.

We all know that Jesus was born, lived, ministered, and died under Roman rule and He introduced the spiritual kingdom of God. Rome persecuted the people of God, both Christians and Jews. But when secular Rome fell, the Church came to power. The church began to gain empire-wide prominence under Constantine and became the government after him.[1]

But go back and look a Daniel's vision (Dan.7), you will notice that the fourth beast has 10 horns, plus a little horn with a mouth speaking blasphemous things. What does this mean?

Christians believe the fourth beast, Rome, will have a second appearance. In other words, there will be a revival of the Roman Empire in our time. Take notice that this 10-horn beast is the same as the 10-horn beast of Revelation 13. The 10-horns symbolizes a coalition of nations led by the little powerful horn who is the Antichrist himself. Again, this is the final gentile world power under the Antichrist who is the proxy for Satan.

Further observe that what Daniel sees next in the same vision is the kingdom of God led by the Messiah, Jesus Christ. It is a forecast of what is to happen in the ends of days, "I saw in the night vision, and behold, with the clouds of heaven there came one like a son of man, and he came to the Ancient of Days and was presented before him. And to him was given dominion and glory and a kingdom, that all peoples, nations, and languages should serve him; his dominion is an everlasting dominion, which shall not pass away and his kingdom, one that shall not be destroyed (Dan.7:13-14). The kingdom of God spoken of here under the Messiah, is positioned to come into head on conflict with the fourth beast with 10 horns plus a little horn (vv.21-22).

Daniel (7:21-27) further explains how the fourth beast makes war with Christ and His people and will be destroyed, but the kingdom of Christ will last forever. In His first advent, Christ made no effort to destroy Rome that was then oppressing Israel and would later persecute the Christian Church. But Christ at His second coming will destroy the revived Roman empire (the fourth beast), the last world empire led by the Antichrist (Dan.7; Rev.13). Jesus then establishes the Kingdom of God upon the earth and rules as the KING of Kings (Rev.19:11-16, 17-21; 20:1-6).

Let's summarize Daniel 7. Daniel's vision saw the Roman empire under which Christ was born, lived, ministered, and died; he also saw the people of God being persecuted by Rome. He further saw the revived Roman empire under the antichrist; the same fourth beast with emphasis upon the 10-horns plus the little horn (same as Rev.13). Christ will destroy this beast (world government) and his kingdom at His second coming (2Thess.2:1-12; Rev.19:11-21).

Daniel saw the big picture in one narrative but did not see or understand the details as we in the Christian era see it. We can clearly look back on the first coming of the Christ: His birth, His upbringing, His ministry, and His death for our redemption. We can also see His second coming but with less clarity. Like Daniel, we don't know or understand all the details.

Daniel continues to have visions with more revelations concerning the near future and the distant time of the end. In chapter 9 he saw the end of the 70 years of exile for the Jews in Babylon (and lived to see it come to pass). The Lord revealed distant things to him such as the restoration of Jerusalem, the cutting off of the Messiah, the destruction of the temple, the cessation of sacrifice, the great tribulation period, and the Antichrist's covenant with Israel. Yet, Daniel did not have the clarity about the time of the end that we Christians have today.

God gave more detail revelation to the apostle Paul and the apostle John concerning the second coming of the Christ. Daniel did not see the Church age; he looked pass it to see what Christians refer to as "the Great Tribulation," and "the final Judgment." We know all this because the closing chapter of Daniel's book (chapter 12) gives us this intelligence report:

> And there shall be a time of trouble, such as never been since there was a nation till that time. But all that time your people shall be delivered, everyone whose name shall be found written in the book. And many of those who sleep in the dust of the earth shall awake, some to everlasting life, and some to shame and everlasting contempt. And those who are wise shall shine as the brightness of the sky above; and those who turn many to righteousness, like the stars forever and ever. (Dan..12:1-3)

The time of trouble spoken of here is undoubtedly *the Great Tribulation* period, which is also called, the time of Jacob's Trouble. The reference to resurrection can be clarified with John 5:28. We know from the New Testament (NT) that there will be two main resurrections: the resurrection of Life and the Resurrection of damnation. One begins with the rapture and ends with the tribulation saints (1Thess.4:16-18; Rev.7:9-15); the other takes place after the millennium in the context of the *Final Judgment* (Rev.20:11-15).

The Prophet Joel **(2:28-3:21)**

The prophet Joel speaks of the repentance and restoration of Israel in the last days (2:28-32). These verses cover the church age to the near ending of *the Great Tribulation*. The last days began with the Resurrection of Jesus Christ (John 11:24-26). The resurrection of the Christ is a *last-days* event; His resurrection is the firstfruits of the last days resurrection (1Cor.15:20-23).

The modern state of Israel is also restored (1948) in the Church age but that restoration is not yet complete because a spiritual turning to God must also occur to complete that restoration process. In chapter 2:28-29, Joel speaks of God's Spirit being poured out on all flesh in the last days; this began at Pentecost, Peter referred to Joel's prophecy (Acts 2:1-8,14-21). Wonders and signs in the heavens will largely take place during the *Great Tribulation* period (Matt.24:29-30; Rev.6:12-17).

Joel also prophesied of God's judgment upon the gentile nations for their treatment of Israel (3:1-17). "For in those days and at that time, when I restore the fortunes of Judah and Jerusalem, I will gather all the nations and bring them down to the Valley of Jehoshaphat. And I will enter into judgment with them there, on behalf of my people and my heritage Israel, because they have scattered them among the nations and have divided up my land..."

(vv.1-3 ESV). Here is one reason Israel is not to be pressured to give up their covenant land; God will judge all such nations that do.

All this will take place at the second advent of the Christ in the context of the Armageddon war and what some Bible scholars refer to as "the judgment of nations" (Matt.25:31-46).

Joel saw some events in the Church age up to what Christians refer to as the second coming of the Christ. But like the other prophets, he saw some last days events and the coming of the Messiah, but did not see the details or understand he was looking at two comings of the Messiah. For him it was one narrative, the coming of the Lord.

The Prophet Zechariah (Chapters 12-14)

The book of Zechariah has some of the most dramatic scenes about the coming of the Lord, we will briefly reference chapters 12 to 14). But we should first note that the nation of Israel has remained a preoccupation of the nations of the world.

For whatever reason, most nations hate Israel, and had it not been for the unwavering support of the United States, perhaps she would not have survived until now. Or, it could be the other way around, the U.S. would not have survived without supporting Israel. God blesses nations that stand with Israel; it is a divine set up (Gen.12:1-3).

Through Zachariah, God has some frightening things to say to the nations of the world about Jerusalem and Israel, "Behold, I am about to make Jerusalem a cup of staggering to all the surrounding peoples. The siege of Jerusalem will also be against Judah. On that day I will make Jerusalem a heavy stone for all peoples. All who lift it will surely hurt themselves. All the nations of the earth will gather against it..."(Zach.12:2-4).

Chapter 13 speaks of the cleansing and salvation of Jerusalem, and chapter 14 shows the visible return of the Christ as He touches down on the Mount of Olives, dividing the mountain into two halves, creating a great valley between where He fights the nations and tramples them under His feet, gaining victory for Israel. It is at this time all Israel will embrace Jesus as their long looked for Messiah. Jesus returns in the nick of time to rescue them from being annihilated by the arm forces of the Antichrist.

Jesus will then sit on the throne of David and rule over the earth for a thousand years (Isaiah 9:6-7; Rev.20:1-10). This is the restoration of the Davidic kingdom that the disciples and Israel wanted so badly when He came the first time. At that time Jesus refused because He wanted to establish redemptive rule in the hearts of people first. God had promised king David that someone will always sit on his throne. The Messiah, Jesus Christ is from the lineage of David (Luke 2:1-7).

Summary

This chapter could have been given the title, *The Return of the Christ: A Fulfillment of Prophecy*. We showed that the OT prophets spoke of *"the coming the Messiah"* as a baby born of a Virgin, dying to redeem His people, and finally delivering them from their human enemies and giving them justice.

But these prophets did not realize that there would have been two comings of the Messiah: one to die providing salvation for His people (John 3:16), and a second coming to literally sit on the throne of David to rule over the earth in justice, righteous and peace (Isaiah 9:6-7).

The leaders of Judaism during the time of Christ could not accept this, so they ended up rejecting the Messiah and had Him executed. To this present time (2023) Israel as a nation has not accepted Jesus Christ. They are still waiting for His first coming, while Christians are waiting for His second coming. The prophets of the OT did not understand the notion of the Messiah coming twice. Judaism to this day stuck with that misunderstanding.

Individual Jews throughout all of Church history have embraced Jesus as their Messiah; today we call them messianic Jews but as a nation Israel has not embraced Christ as their Messiah. They are still waiting for Him. To their surprise, He will be none other but Jesus of Nazareth whom they have rejected all this time. Imagine how different their history could have been.

CHAPTER 2

THE PURPOSE OF CHRIST RETURNING TO EARTH

Christ's first advent to earth was not a pleasant visit for Him. He was not born at the Metropolitan Hospital birthing suite. His mother was not given accommodations at a five-star hotel.

His birth was in a manger (Luke 2:1-7). But He did not allow His lowly birth to hinder Him from accomplishing His assigned life's mission nor should you. Don't allow the circumstances of your birth and upbringing to hinder the development of your God-given potential or your purpose in life. None of us came into this world by accident but by divine decree. God wants us here!

People today, in their quest for respectability and status would want to keep the manger thing quiet. But God broadcast it on the front pages of Scripture and made it theatrical scenes throughout the ages. It reminds us that each of us has a story, and that story is special. It is your story; it is my story!

In His first advent, Jesus was rejected by His own people (John 1:12). It is not that they did not know He was coming. Priests and prophets from Moses to John the Baptist announced His coming; they named to what lineage and tribe He would be connected, and the city He would be born (Micah 5:2). Prophets heralded the circumstances under which the Messiah would arrive: Virgin born, Son of David, tribe of Judah (Isa.7:14-16; 9:1-7).

On the very night of the Messiah's birth, Shepherds on a Judean hillside were personally and immediately informed by heaven through angelic messengers. They promptly handed off their flocks to servants and went to Bethlehem to visit the newborn King (Luke 2:7-20). His arrival was no secret!

Strangers from afar were also notified by cosmic signs that a King was born; following a star, they travelled long and far to pay homage (Matt.2:1-12). But the strange and troubling irony is this-- Israel's religious leaders stayed home. They were not even moved out of curiosity to investigate the matter as others did!

We cannot excuse the religious leaders on the grounds of ignorance, that they did not know. They were the ones who gave the murderous King Herod the information where the Christ child would be born (Matt.2: 4-6). They were summons to His palace in the dead of night, anywhere between 1:00 to 4:00 a.m.

Herod demanded of them what the Hebrew prophets said about the Christ child. But he did so under the pretense of wanting to go and worship him as Messiah and King. They turned to their scrolls of the Hebrew Scriptures and provided him the information. Herod's soldiers used the information to conduct a murderous campaign, slaughtering the children of Bethlehem in their effort to kill the Christ child. And Israel's religious leaders went back to bed. We know this, because the star the Magi followed was still brightly ablaze in the night sky (Matt.2:2, 9).

Israel's religious leaders were not ignorant men. They were the intelligentsia, the elite class, the teachers of their people, men with resources at their command. They heard that their long-awaited Messiah has finally arrived; this means, the liberation and redemption of Israel was at hand, and the information awakened nothing in them; they went back to bed. Or, should I say, they remained asleep! This attitude is not benign; it is a spiritual malignancy that will metastasized into full blown rejection.

The callousness of heart, the spiritual blindness of these religious leaders increasingly got worst. A priest circumcised the child when he was eight days old; later he was blessed in the temple by a priest in Jerusalem where marvelous revelations were given about the child and His mother by several people (Luke 2: 22-40). Even if one were blind, dumb, and deaf these signs of the Messiah would be hard to miss; this is willful ignorance.

At age 12, the brilliance, the wisdom, and insight of the boy Jesus stunned these learned religious leaders, experts in the Law and the entire Hebrew Bible (Luke 2: 41-52). Amidst all this nothing aroused their suspicion that this boy might be the Messiah. What else could this be but willful blindness?

The boy grew up and called them, "blind guides," "hypocrites," "blind fools" (Matt.23: 16-25). These labels are well deserved, appropriate descriptions of their spiritual condition long prophesied by Isaiah the prophet (6: 9-12).

The boy grew up and told them repeatedly over a three-year period that He is the Messiah. He confirmed His identity in preaching, teaching, and in mighty miraculous deeds that no one before Him had ever done. He cast out demons, healed the sick, raised the dead, turned water into wine, walked on water, fed over five thousand people with a little boy's lunch, and returned a borrowed tomb three days after His funeral. Yet, they rejected Him and had the Romans hung Him high and stretch Him wide on a cross until He was dead. He rose from the dead and they denied the truth and covered the evidence (Matt.28:11-15).Compounded rejection.

If you did so much good for a people and they rejected you to that degree, who among us would return to help them? That alone suggest that this man is unique above the rest of us. Let me add, the generation of rascals that did that to Him is not the ones to whom He is returning. That generation is long dead. But even so, why return? That generation's off springs continue to believe the lies of Caiaphas concerning Jesus of Nazareth to this day. Why is Jesus returning?

To Fulfill Promises Made

Fundamentally, the return of the Christ to earth is to fulfill promises made to His people. His return is a promise kept.

The promise to return was made not only to His immediate disciples, but to all the people of God. That promise sweetens the Christian walk amidst bitter experiences. It is the believers' blessed hope. The certainty of the promise is rooted in the character of the promise-maker and his redemptive works.

It is that certainty of faith that moved the apostle Paul to boldly say, "And we boast in the hope of the glory of God...we glory also in our sufferings, because we know that suffering produces perseverance, perseverance character, and character hope. And hope does not put us to shame, because God's love has been poured out into our hearts through the Holy Spirit who has been given to us" (Rom.5:2- 5). People will endure untold hardship with a promise of much gold or eternal life in the end.

Jesus confidently declared, "In my Father's house are many rooms. If it were not so, would I have told you that I go to prepare a place for you? And if I go and prepare a place for you, I will come again and will take you to myself, that where I am you may be also" (John 14:1-3, 16: 5-7 ESV).

Jesus ascended to heaven forty days after His resurrection (Acts 1:6-9). The angels at the place of ascension affirm that Jesus will return (vv. 10-11). Christians do not normally boast on what the angels say here, but at least, it solidifies confidence that they represent a truth speaking administration. The testimony of the angels reveals that the promise to return has a broader knowledge base than the person of Jesus. Angels don't represent themselves; they are messengers of a higher authority. They were sent.

The arrival of the Holy Spirit ten days after the ascension is another affirmation that Jesus reached His destination; that also is promise fulfilled. His departure from earth and arrival in heaven were made contingent on the coming of Holy Spirit (John 16:7-15).

The visit and message of the ascended Christ to the seven churches of Asia Minor is another confirmation that He did reach heaven safely and His mind is fixed on returning as He confirmed to these churches of the apocalypse of John (Rev.1-3).

All the apostles and the New Testament church understood, accepted, and preached the return of the Christ (1Cor.15:23; 1Thess.4:16-18; I Peter).

Furthermore, Jesus did not have a history of lying, or being untrustworthy, or one prone to deception. The quality of a person's character and integrity is based on the honesty of their word, tested and proven. One who cannot keep his word cannot be trusted. That was never the case with the Lord Jesus; there has never been one case of being untrustworthy in His history.

Our relationship with Jesus Christ is based on faith; Jesus cannot be separated from His Word. Speaking of the second person of the Trinity, the apostle John gives us this intelligence report, "In the beginning was the Word, and the Word was with God, and the Word was God." The Word became incarnate and dwell among us (John 1:1, 14). The Christ is one with His word.

If Jesus wanted to backout of the redemption business—one opportune time was when Satan offered Him the kingdoms of the world and the glory of then, but Jesus rejected Satan's bold offer (Matt.4:8-11). Gethsemane was another opportune to change His mind and backout, but He did not (Matt.26 36-46). Frankly, the matter was settled from eternity "by the determinate counsel and foreknowledge of God" (Acts 2:23 KJV).

Finally, the worth of a promise is no better than the character of the person who made it. In former decades, people would say, my word is good for it, and they would shake hands but in these last days, people fail to honor even written contracts.

Trustworthiness speaks to a person's character. The character of God is seen from the opening chapters of Genesis, and it remains constant to the closing chapter of Revelation. God's Word stands;

He is faithful! His Word to us are not suggestions, but executive orders to obey; they speak to His holy character.

The God of the Old Covenant is the God of the New. His redemption plan to humankind unfolds in His Word; it is reliable and dependable. The reality of His coming at the end of the age was foretold by the prophets as shown in chapter one of this book. God is a covenant maker and a covenant keeper; a covenant keeper is the same as a promise keeper (Heb.6:13-20). If He does not come back in keeping with His promise, He would be an imposter.

To Fulfill Prophecy (OT)

Christ returns to earth to fulfill numerous Old Testament (OT) prophecies. Just about every OT prophet prophesied about the coming of the Lord; some of those prophecies were fulfilled in Christ first advent, but many are applicable to His second advent and are awaiting fulfillment. And they must come to pass!

No word spoken by God the Father, Jesus Christ or the blessed Holy Spirit can be taken lightly. They are executive orders to obey, not suggestions to ignore. Every word of God is connected to a purpose that must be fulfilled (Isa. 55:10-11). Jesus declares in His Sermon on the Mount, "Do not think that I have come to abolish the Law or the Prophets; I have not come to abolish them but to fulfill them" (Matt.5:17). He goes on to say, "...not the smallest letter, nor the least stroke of a pen, will by any means disappear from the Law until everything is accomplished" (v.18).

This means, whatever scripture passage of the Hebrew Bible that was not fulfilled during the first advent of the Christ or during the Church age, must still be fulfilled upon the second advent of the Christ. God does not speak into the air, nor does His words fall to the ground accomplishing nothing.

As the Believers' Hope Realized

The return of the Christ to earth is the blessed hope of the people of God realized as well as the entire created order. It is God declaring to all humankind and the cosmos that He is the true creator, landlord, and owner. He redeems both, man and cosmos.

Titus expresses it this way, "For the grace of God has appeared bringing salvation for all people. It teaches to say, 'No' to ungodliness and worldly passions, and live self-controlled, upright, and godly lives in this present age, while we wait for the blessed hope—the glory appearing of our great God and Savior, Jesus Christ..." (Titus 2:11-13).

The return of the Christ is a vindication of the righteous who have suffered so much in the name of the Lord. It is also a vindication of Jesus Christ who was treated horribly during His first advent. His enemies knew He was innocent but had Him crucified out of malice. They denied and covered truth of His resurrection, and declared the Christian church a lie and Jesus an imposter.

The true people of God have been declared and manifested to the heavenly community, and now they declared to the earthly communities of unbelievers (Matt.24:29-31). Their leaders, the Antichrist and the False prophet will be captured and thrown into the eternal lake of burning sulfur (Rev.19:19-20). And millions of unbelievers will be slaughtered, and the birds of prey will feed on their carcasses (v.21). Satan, their lord and master will be incarcerated for a thousand years (Rev.20:1-3). Yes, this is the blessed hope of believers realized and vindicated.

Once we the children of God are manifested and our status declared to the unbelieving world, the curse will be lifted off creation. I am speaking of the curse that was levied upon creation by reason of the fall of our ancestral patients in the Paradise Garden. They compromised with Satan and the whole creation was dragged down with them. God said to Adam, "Because you listen to your wife and ate fruit from the tree...I commanded you not to eat...cursed is the ground because of you; through painful toil you will eat food from it all the days of your life..." (Gen.3:17-19). From that time the whole creation has been groaning and travailing in pain until now. But now the whole creation is ready for deliverance from the curse. The apostle Paul said it best:

> For the creation waits in eager expectation for the children of God to be revealed. For the creation was subjected to frustration, not by its own choice, but by the will of the one who subjected it, in hope that the creation itself will be liberated from its bondage to decay and brought into the freedom and glory of the children of God. We know that the whole creation has been groaning as in the pains of childbirth right up to the present time. Not only so, but we ourselves, who have the firstfruits of the Spirit, groan inwardly as we wait eagerly for our adoption to sonship, the redemption of our bodies. For in this hope, we were saved....(Rom. 8: 19-25)

The believers' adoption has been finalized, we are in our new bodies and in our state of glorification. We have been declared to the heavenly community by the Son to the Father. The Father has declared us to all heaven as His children. We celebrated the *Marriage Supper of the Lamb,* and now we have returned with Christ to earth to put down His enemies and to reign.

Our return to earth with Christ is the final declaration that we are the children of God; this is a declaration to the unbelieving earth community and perhaps the god of this world and his demons. This means, all the conditions spoken of in the preceding Scripture quotation have been met. It is time for the curse to be lifted off creation, so we can entire the millennial reign of Christ over the earth with that curse gone.

It is because the curse has been lifted, the lion and the lamb can lie down together, and a little child can lead them. Humans waring against each other is officially over, so nation can convert any leftover war equipment into agricultural instruments (Isa.2:4).

The creation has been waiting for the manifestation of the children of God and that realization has now come to fruition. The wait is over! Faith in the Lord Jesus Christ has paid off beyond our wildest dreams and expectations. Thanks to the blessed Holy Spirit for His work with us believers from conversion to glorification!

To Put Down All Oppositions

God and His Kingdom have been long opposed by Satan and his angels. Then humans joined with Satan against God and His Christ. Satan and his hosts will oppose Jesus to the end; he will assert his power as god over this earth, and try to prevent Jesus from returning to reign. That is what the unholy trinity is all about, that is: Satan, the Antichrist, and the False prophet (Rev.13:1-18).

But Jesus will destroy their armies, throw the Antichrist and the False prophet into hell, and put Satan in prison for a thousand years. Later, Jesus will throw Satan into hell where his friends were previously thrown (Rev.19:19-21,20:1-3,7-10). From the time of His resurrection, Christ was given all authority in heaven and earth, and He will put down all opposition to His authority (Philip.2: 9-11).

To Judge the Nations

All the nations under the Antichrist leadership that are gathered in the Middle East to annihilate Israel will be judged by Christ including Israel. This is referred to in the literature as the judgment of nation of which Christ Himself speaks of during the week of His passion (Matt.25:31-46). This is part of Christ putting down all opposition to His authority as indicated in the previous section.

Some scholars think the judgment of nations is the final judgment that will take place after the millennium. But that notion can be countered by the fact that since the Antichrist and the False prophet who are Satan's human proxies, governmental and military leaders are judged and thrown into hell immediately upon Christ's return, it follows that the millions of soldiers and support personnel would be judged at the same time. These are judged as living flesh and blood humans. They cannot enter the millennium.

Since Jesus arrived to rescue Israel from annihilation, it follows that as a nation they will be judged for their rejection of the Messiah until now. Of course, at this time Israel will finally accept the Jesus as their Messiah, so all Israel will be saved (Rom.11 25-32). This remnant of Israel that embrace Jesus as the Messiah at this time will enter the millennium with Him to reign. (See Volumes 6 & 7 "Armageddon" and the "Millennium" for details.

To Reign Over the Earth

Christ returns to reign over the earth. Isaiah prophesied, "For to us a child is born, to us a son is given, and the government will be on his shoulders. And he will be called Wonderful Counselor, Mighty God, Everlasting Father, Prince of Peace. Of the greatness of his government and peace there will be no end. He will reign on David's throne and over his kingdom, establishing and upholding it with justice and righteousness from that time on and forever. The zeal of the Lord Almighty will accomplish this" (Isa.9:6-7).

The preceding prophecy will be fulfilled when Christ returns, put down all opposing authorities to His kingdom and His covenant land, then He will begin His rule over the earth.

The Lord Jesus Christ sat on no earthly throne nor headed any earthly government during His first advent. He told the Roman governor; "my kingdom is not of this world" (John 18:36). The preceding Scripture quote from Isaiah is yet to be fulfilled, and it will be upon Christ's return to earth to reign (see Volume 7).

To Judge the Living and the Dead

Christ returns to judge the living and the dead. No human being that has ever lived will escape the judgment of God. This fact is not only evident in both Old and New Testaments, but in major creeds of the Christian Church.[1]

Every soul that has ever lived and died must face resurrection and judgment, and every person that remains alive to the coming of the Lord must face judgment (Dan.12:1-4; John 5:28). So, whether a person lives or dies, he or she must be judged to receive his or her just due. So, a person has not escaped judgment because he dies; he may escape human justice but not God's.

The resurrection of the Christ guarantees a resurrection of life and a resurrection of damnation (John 5:28; Rev. 20:11-15). Everybody will not be resurrected and judged at the same time, but when it is all over everyone will be judged.

This author maintains that all righteous people of the Old and New Testament eras will be resurrected at once with the saints of the Church age at the rapture. But there are others who believe that OT saints will be resurrected separately from Church folks. The latter seems more like a dispensational theological position.

We must bear in mind that not all OT saints are Israelites, neither are all NT saints gentiles. Both groups are a mixed multitude. But God has one redemption plan for all humankind and that is through Jesus Christ and His cross (John 3:16).

But even if NT believers are resurrected at the rapture and OT at the second coming of Christ, both groups of righteous people will face judgment, one group in heaven and the other on earth. All unbelievers will face Judgment just the same. No one will escape being judge, righteous or unrighteous, Jew or Gentile.

The Judgment is the Supreme Court of God Almighty. Some sessions will be in heaven immediately after the rapture, and some session after He returns to the earth, and the final sessions after the millennium. The Final Judgment is at the end of the millennium (Rev.20:11-15).

There are only two judgment categories, one corresponds with the resurrection of life and the other the resurrection of damnation. One judgment category is based upon works for the purpose of rewards, and the other judgment category for person's sin and condemnation (2 Cor.5:10; Rev.20:11-15).

Righteousness, truth, and justice constitute the foundation of God's throne. Therefore, ever wrong must be corrected, every unjust deed punished and the innocent vindicated (See volume 2 The Believer's Judgment, and volume 9 The Final Judgment).

To Establish the New World Order

Ambitious world leaders have been talking about a new world order for some time as if human ingenuity will bring it about. The idea is barrowed from the Bible but sinful humans will not be able to bring it about by themselves, no matter how hard they try. Human history is one of warfare, killing each other. After World War I nations got together and pledge, never again. But did we live in peace and prosperity or planned another World War?

God Himself will bring about the New World order after Jesus Christ complete a thousand years of peaceful reign over the earth as its KING of Kings and LORD of Lords. This period is called the millennium. At the end of the millennium there will be Final Judgment. The wicked dead of all ages will come to life again and be judged for the sins they committed while they were first alive in the body. They will be given their just due by joining Satan in the lake of burning sulfur (Rev.20:11-15).

After all evils and opposing authorities are vanquished from God's creation, there will be a new heaven and earth. The New Capital and administrative City of God will be the New Jerusalem (Rev. 21-22). This will be the New World Order.

It will be a theocracy, a government under God Almighty. It will be a world where dwells righteousness; evil will be forever done away with, and God's Kingdom will full all things and God will dwell with His people (See Volume 10).

CHAPTER 3

WHEN WILL CHRIST RETURN?

Every time the question of "when will Christ return" is asked, the first response you are likely to get is a statement made by Jesus in His Olivet discourse that no man or angel knows the day and hour of His coming, not even the Son of Man, only the Father (Matt. 24: 36). Yet in that same discourse Jesus gives us signs of His coming, and states explicitly that He would return immediately after the t*ribulation* of those days (vv.29-31).

Are these two statements contradicting each other? The answer is no! But the matter requires some critical thinking and explaining. In this chapter we will look at signs of the return of the Christ and unpack the two seemingly contradictory statements.

Jesus provided signs of His return in response to a question asked by His disciples about the signs of His return and the end of the age. They proposed the question after Jesus gave a prophecy concerning the destruction of the Jewish temple. They had just left the temple and were showing Jesus the magnificence and this imposing structure. But to their surprise Jesus said there is coming a day went not one stone will be left upon another that shall not be thrown down (Matt.24:1-2). The destruction of the temple would mean the dismantling of Judaism, shocking to His disciples.

This temple was a gift from Herod the Great to the Jews. It was larger and more elegant than previous temples. It took over 80 years to complete; construction started about B.C. 20 and ended about 63 A.D.[1] Some stones were 40 feet long white marble, some overlaid with gold.[2] It is said to have been the tallest building in Jerusalem; its golden doom was the first to catch the sunlight of the rising sun each morning and the last to reflect the light of the setting sun. It was no ordinary structure.

Jewish life in first century A.D. and prior, revolved around the Torah, sacrifice, and the temple; all three were needed to worship Yahweh appropriately. The temple was the central meeting place for Jewish life; it was the only place that sacrifices could be offered. So, it must have been a shock to the disciples when Jesus predicted the destruction of the temple; it meant the end of Judaism as they knew it. It was a corrupted, self-serving system.

The Roman army destroyed Jerusalem and the temple in 70 A.D. as prophesied; no temple has been built to take its place since. Judaism today is a post-A.D.70 reinvention, without sacrifice, without the temple, without the Ark of the Covenant, and without the shekinah glory of God. We will now look at signs of Christ return.

Signs of Christ's Return

It is against the preceding background that the disciples came privately to Jesus as He was sitting on the Mount of Olives overlooking Jerusalem and asked, "when will these things be, and what will be the sign your coming, and of the end of the age?" (Matt.24:1-3). Jesus answered both questions: 1) the time of the destruction of Jerusalem and the temple, and 2) the signs of His return and end of the age. The answer concerning His return is extensive; that answer is our focus here.

The signs Jesus gave will occur between His ascension and His return. One may say, these events always happen in human history. That is true, but they will become increasingly wider in scope intensity to alarming levels not seen before.

First, there will be widespread religious deception, false messiahs. Jesus warned, "Take heed that no one deceives you. For many will come in my name, saying, I am the Christ, and will deceive many (Matt.24:4, 11; Luke 21:8-9). Judaism has witnessed many false messiahs since this prophecy was given. There must be a reason religious deception is placed first—this is the area that believers and unbelievers are most vulnerable for being taken captives and lead away.

Satan is the master deceiver; he dresses in religious attire, and he speaks religiously. He can transform himself to look like an angel of light when playing the role of deceiver. Worship is what he wants most of all, and he will do anything to get it. He will lie, bribe, steal, kill and destroy to achieve his goal (John 10:10a).

Second, Jesus warns of wars and rumors of war (talk about wars) (Matt.24:6-7; Luke 21:7-10). Now adays, the word war is attached to many ordinary words: political war, drug war, economic war, cold war, race war, and so on. But that which terrifies people most is nuclear war. Since Russia's war with Ukraine, there has been much threat of one side using nuclear weapons to achieve what it is unable to achieve conventionally. This threat of nuclear holocaust is terrifying for most people.

The nuclear powers have agreed not use nuclear weapons because it is unwinnable, and the outcome will be mutual destruction and national suicide. But despite the agreement, people lie, and nations violate treaties before. It takes only one mad man to plunge the world into unwanted nuclear war. We the people of God know war will intensify as earth counts down to Armageddon, but humans will not be allowed to destroy the earth. But we can cause whole lot of damage, life hell for all.

Third, Jesus warned that there will be famine, pestilence, and earthquake in various places (Matt.24:7; Luke 21:11). Famine speaks of global food shortages due to war, pestilences, and natural disasters. Pests and diseases can become pandemic, destroying vegetation, and worsen food shortages. Climate change and war will also serve as major contributors to global food shortage such as the world has never seen.

Earthquake will increase in intensity causing volcanic eruptions, rising seas, and tsunamis. Life will increasingly become unbearable upon the earth. These conditions will reach their maximum intensity during a seven-year period Bible scholars label, *the Great Tribulation* as the seven seal judgments of Revelation (5-6) is administered.

Fourth, Jesus warned of growing religious intolerance and persecution. "You will be hated by all nations for my name's sake" (Matt.24:9-10; 21:12-13). Followers of Jesus Christ will be hated, and there will be state sponsored persecution as it was during the Roman empire but on a larger and more intense scale. This is already being experienced across the world but will get worst with the rise of the Antichrist and the False prophet (Rev.13).

Five, lawlessness will abound (Matt.24:12). Lawlessness does not mean there is no law, but there will be reckless disregard for the law, making the January 6th capitol insurrection look like a picnic. The apostle Paul speaks about a lawless personality that will take control of world government and become a law unto himself; in fact, the only law (2 Thess. 2: 1-12).

Sixth, there will be a great fallen away from the faith, apostasy (2 Thess.2). This falling away includes a false church with false preachers and teachers whose motivation is the unrighteous mammon. This false system which is now taking shape is represented by a prostitute riding a ten-horn beast with a communion challis in her hand (Rev.17:1-18).

Jesus said, because iniquity shall abound, the love of many shall wax cold (Matt.24:12). In other words, churches and Individuals who were once fervent believers have cooled off from their spirituality to become backslidden and spiritually dead. The Church across the world is already showing alarming symptoms of this backslidden condition.

Seventh, there will be ecology unrest in nature, signs in the sky as the powers of the heavens will be shaken. Disasters will intensify everywhere (Luke 21:25-26). Planet earth is already seeing these near apocalyptic disasters manifesting.

The Day and Hour of Christ's Return

Despite the signs given to warn us of the nearness of Christ return, the exact time remains classified, unknown to humans and angels. Jesus Himself said, "but of that day and hour knows no man, not the angels of heaven or the Son of Man, only the Father" (Matt.24:36). "The Son of Man" refers to Jesus Himself.

You may be thinking, how is it that Jesus does not know the time of His own return? Sounds confusing, does it? Let us try to clear this up before we proceed.

First, Jesus was not speaking as God when he made the statement, but as man. As a man, he did not know because like us His knowledge would have been limited. But now that He is glorified and exalted with all the attributes of deity restored, we can confidently say, He knows! The time of His return is fixed; the information is classified and known only to the Holy Trinity.

Just in case you are still puzzled. Let us take another go at it. To become man, the second person of the Trinity had to lay aside His glory (that is, a brightness more intense than the sun in the sky). That glory includes His majesty, and by extension the exercise of certain attributes belonging to God only, such as omnipresence, omniscience, and omnipotence (Philip.2:5-8). So, as a man Jesus did not exercise all the God quality of knowing everything or being all-powerful or being able to be present everywhere at once. He became a human person like you and me but was sinless.

He took on the exercise of these attributes again sometime after His resurrection or ascension or at His exaltation (vv.9-11). In fact, in His High Priestly prayer, Jesus requested of the Father the restoration of His previous glory (John 17:1-5, 24).

Second, note that the Scripture did not say, of that year no one knows; it says, "of that day and hour." Should we take the words of Jesus that literal? Yes, these words should be taken literally because, technically speaking, the year of Jesus return can be calculated but only after the rapture takes place. So, the statement was intended for the event called, the rapture. The rapture is often spoken of in the context of the second coming.

In other word, Jesus hardly speaks of the rapture separately from His second coming; the two events were always lumped together in the same narrative. So, scripture passages that likens the coming of the Lord to a thief in the night, unexpected, unannounced are more sharply applicable to the rapture.

Jesus gave us the approximate time of His return by naming several signs to look for; He did not intend His Second Coming to be a secret (Matt.24). He wants the unbeliever to be saved urgently and the believers to be watchful, in a state of readiness.

In Volume 1 of this series, it is stated that the rapture is rigidly imminent. That means, the Lord can call for His people anytime. For that reason, we cannot calculate the year, month, week, day, hour or second that the rapture will happen. Believers are warned to be in a state of constant readiness and watchfulness that they are not taken by surprise. This is the event that should motivate unbelievers to become believers urgently because if they miss this event their chances of being saved will be extremely difficult.

However, throughout the history of the Church people have attempted to calculate and set dates but they have all failed to date. But after the rapture takes place, we know that the people of God will be gone from the earth for the seven years of *Great Tribulation* and will return with Jesus "immediately after the tribulation of those days" (Matt.24: 29-31). In fact, Jesus returns with His people to end the *Great Tribulation*.

Just before His return, the people of God are seen in heaven celebrating with Him (Rev.19:1-8). If they are in heaven, how did they get there? They are there because Jesus called for them in the event commonly referred to as the rapture (1Thess.4:16-18). Believers are also seen leaving heaven with Jesus on His return to earth, shortly after the *Marriage Supper* (Rev.19:11-21).

So, after the rapture has occurred, a third grader can calculate the year that Christ will return to earth because the Bible says He returns "immediately after the tribulation of those days" but more accurately to end the tribulation (Matt.24:29-30). The tribulation is seven years, it begins with the rapture and ends with Jesus returning and defeating the Antichrist's armies.

But calculating the Lord's return at that time is of little or no benefit to unbelievers because they already missed the most important event, the rapture. Unbeliever's can get saved during the tribulation but at the cost of their own lives.

At the risk of being redundant—the warning of no one knowing the day and hour of the Lord's return, is directed to the people of God and is more applicable to the rapture event. But even though the world of unbelievers will be able to calculate the approximate time of Christ's return after the rapture takes place, chances are His return will still take them unawares, just as Noah's generation was warned but did not believe until disaster swept them all away (Matt.24:36-39).

Unbelievers will continue to do what unbelievers do, even when they can calculate the time. They will be too busy partying rather than paying attention to the time of the Lord's return. Furthermore, if they already taken the mark of the beast their chance of being saved is forever loss (Rev.13:8; 20:4). That said, many unbelievers will be saved after the rapture; they are called, tribulation saints. Why is the date of the Lord's return now classified or unknown?

Knowing the date would not make a big difference to unbelievers, they would just wait and see and get left just the same. Furthermore, the Lord wants His people to be at their assignment while watching for His call from heaven (1Thess.4:16-18). So be ready for in such an hour when you think not the Son of Man will call for you (Matt.24: 42-44). Unbelievers should heed the gospel message and become believers that they too can be included in the rapture crowd.

When the Gospel is Fully Preached

Another important marker of the return of the Christ is the *evangelization of the world.* In His response to the disciples' question, "what shall be the sign of thy coming and of the end of the age?" Jesus added this statement, "And this gospel of the kingdom will be preached in the whole world as a testimony to all nations and then the end will come" (Matt.24:24).

This is a very important key to the "when" of Christ's return. There is a mission task to be completed before He comes. And only the blessed Holy Trinity knows when that task is satisfactorily completed. So, the people of God must not become preoccupied with dates and time but be about the task of world evangelization while in a state of watchfulness and readiness.

The first advent of the Christ was to provide salvation through His substitutionary sacrifice on the cross for all humankind (Isaiah 53: 4-12; John 3:16; Romans 5:1-8). But how are humans all over the world to get this good news (gospel) that their sin debt is paid in full? Jesus Christ put a three-part plan in place to get this information out to peoples of all nations before He returns.

First, He established a global enterprise that no earthly powers can destroy; it is called the Church (Matt.16: 17-19). This divine enterprise is not built upon failing, fragile mortals as Peter, but upon Jesus Himself who is the Chief foundation stone of the Church (Eph.2:19-22; 1Peter 2:4-10). This does not mean the witness of the individual or local congregation cannot be compromised and removed. The lampstand or witness of a compromising, backslidden local church can be removed if that church refuses to repent and represent Christ properly (Rev.2:5).

But the Church itself as a global enterprise is indestructible. Humans, Satan, or the gates of hell cannot destroy the Church; the Church also has the power to bind and loose with the authority of heaven (Matt.16:18-19). The Church is that spiritually transformed, Holy Spirit empowered community to whom Jesus entrusted the gospel (Acts 1:8, 2:1-4). When Jesus ascended to heaven the size of the community was only 120 persons; that is the number we can speak of for sure (Acts 1:9-15). With the agency of the blessed Holy

Spirit, the Church has grown from that mustard seed size to over 2.38 billion in 2022, and perhaps much more.

Second, the Lord of the Church issues an executive order that has become the mission statement of His enterprise, the Church. Here is the executive order:

> All authority in heaven and on earth has been given to me. Therefore, go and make disciples of all nations, baptizing them in the name of the Father and of the Son and of the Holy Spirit, and teaching them to obey everything I have commanded you. And surely, I am with you always, to the end of the age. (Matt.28:18-20)

Note the segments :1) Go, make disciples, activity: preaching, teaching, winning, training, enlisting. 2) Baptizing, teaching to obey, nurturing, caring, discipling. Making disciples is much more than winning people to Christ; it is also teaching them to obey what Jesus commanded, nurture them, and enlist them to serve.

The primary task of the Church is not to win the approximately 8 billion people in the world to Jesus Christ, but to ensure that all nations hear the gospel of God's saving grace. We know that some individuals will be saved, but we do not know who they are, so me must urgently get the gospel out to all nations. With the help of broadcast mass media, social media, the internet, and the print media the goal of reaching every nation should not be far off. Neither is the return of Jesus Christ far off.

Third, the product of the enterprise is the good news; in short, the gospel. Every enterprise, be it Apple, Google or Amazon has at least one product it brings to the marketplace. Some people want the Church to involve itself in everything, but that is not its mission.

Our product is the gospel, and it should not be diluted. Persons that bring the product of the gospel to others, must be first transformed by it and worthy of the name preacher or teacher from a biblical perspective.

It is the preacher/teacher who is called to announced or proclaim to all nations the gospel in keeping with the executive order given by the Lord of the Church. The apostle Paul reminds us, "Everyone who calls on the name of the Lord will be saved." But they must first hear and believe, and a preacher must be called and sent with the gospel for the unbeliever to hear and believe (Rom. 10:13-15). Christ will return when the gospel is preached as a witness to all nations.

Day of the Lord Vs the Day of Christ

The Bible speaks of the "Day of Lord" and the "Day of Christ;" they are not the same, so don't confuse one with the other.[1] The Day of Christ denotes what we generally refer to as the rapture, the time that Christ calls for and removes His people out of harm's way to heaven (1Thess.4:16-18). Paul declares, "For God has not appointed us unto wrath, but to obtain salvation by our Lord Jesus Christ...." (1 Thess.5: 9 KJV).

Salvation is deliverance from something hurtful. It is often used in association to sin, delivered from sin or saved from sin. Here it is used in reference to the time God rescues His people from the wrath of the *Great Tribulation.* It is the time the Lamb of God pours out His wrath upon the unbelieving world and cut back on the resources of the earth that make people comfortable in their rebellion against God. The Lamb, the Son of God is seen administering these judgments or calamities in the breaking of the seven-seal scroll of Revelation (Rev.5-6).

Paul prayed for the Corinthian believers that God would keep them "firm to the end" so that they will be "blameless on the day of our Lord Jesus Christ" (1Cor.1:8). The term is also used in other passages (2 Cor.1 14; Phil.1: 6, 2:16).

The Day of the LORD is more frequently used in the Old Testament but not as frequent in the New. It is refers to "a protracted period commencing with the second advent of Christ in glory and ending with the cleansing of the heavens and the earth by fire preparatory to the new heavens and the new earth of the eternal state" (Isa.65: 17-19; 66: 22; 2 Thess.2: 2; 2 Peter3: 13; Rev.21: 1).[2] During this time God is visible upon the earth for all to see (Rev.22:3-4).

Summary

In as much as Christ has not given a specific date of for His return, He has given numerous signs that we can know when His coming is at hand. It is an excise in futility for believers or unbelievers to burden themselves calculating the date and time of His return.

The foundational issue is, do you want to submit your life to the Lordship of Christ and serve the cause of His Kingdom? Then do so in a state of readiness and watchfulness. That is the way the Lord wants us to do it (Matt.24: 42-51). There is no fix date for the rapture and calculate it is futile.

To the unbeliever or seeker, Jesus Himself said, seek first the kingdom of God and His righteousness and the other benefits you seek will be given to you. Getting into the kingdom should be the priority of those who are outside, not worrying about dates and time (John 3:1-5, 16). No one will be able to calculate the date of Christ return until after the Church is raptured, then what benefit will it be then? You are left here to face the most horrific time humans have ever seen. Your chances for being saved then is little to none (see Volume 3, *The Great Tribulation Survival Guide*...).

People who are busy in the cause Christ and the work of His kingdom do not need to become preoccupied with dates and time, for we already know the Lord is coming back and we need to be in a state of readiness and watchfulness (1Thess.5: 1-4; Matt. 24: 42-46).

CHAPTER 4

HOW WILL CHRIST RETURN?

The return of our Lord Jesus Christ to earth is certain; there is nothing in the created or uncreated universe to stop that event from happening. His coming is sure! Both Old and New Testament saints have prophesied and waited with eager anticipation for the coming of the Kingdom of God.

Many have prayed the famous line from the Lord's Prayer, "thy kingdom come, thy will be done on earth as it is in haven" (Matt.6:10). This line of the prayer is fulfilled when the Christ returns as KING of kings and LORD of lords. This chapter answers the question, "how will He return?"

Christ Returns Personally

Christ is not returning as a phantom or ghost or disembodied spirit; He is coming back as a real, substantive person that you can see, touch, and feel. He will be in the same resurrection body He ascended to heaven with; it is a spiritual body but not ghostly.

Jesus said to Thomas after His resurrection, "Look at my hands and my feet. It is I myself! Touch me and see; a ghost does not have flesh and bone, as you see I have" (Luke 24:36-44). He ascended to heaven in this same body, and He will return in this same body (Acts 1:11; 1John 3:1-2).

There are liberal scholars who do not believe in the personal, bodily return of the Christ; they hold to a spiritual return position of the Lord, akin to the coming of the Holy Spirit. The problem is, the Bible does not teach such. His return body will be substantive.

Jesus promised to His disciples is that of a personal return (John 14:1-4). The angels at the site of ascension affirms that this same Jesus would come again (Acts 1:9-11). The apostle Paul declares, "For the Lord Himself shall descend from heaven with a shout..." (1Thess.4:16). Jude quoted this prophecy of Enoch, "See, the Lord is coming with thousands upon thousands of his holy ones to judge everyone, and to convict all of them of all the ungodly acts they have committed..." (vv.14-15).

Jesus is not sending anyone in His place, and believers are not expecting anyone else but Jesus Himself. He is coming in person! To this end the writer of Hebrews declares, "Christ was offered once to bear the sins of many. To those who eagerly wait for Him,

He will appear a second time, apart from sin, for salvation" (Heb. 9:28 NKJV). The apostle Paul speaks of a "crown of righteousness the Lord, the righteous judge will award to him" on that special day, and not to him only, "but also to all who have longed for his appearing" (2 Tim.4: 8).

One of the oldest Patriarchs of the Bible that ever lived is Job. He prophesied in the predicament of his suffering the following:

> For I know my Redeemer lives, and that He shall stand on the earth; and after my skin is destroy, this I know, that in my flesh I shall see God, whom I shall see for myself, and my eyes shall behold, and not another. How my heart yearns within me! (Job 19:25-27 NKJV).

Job did not know the name Jesus or Christ as we now know these names, nor did he possess the clarity of the Holy Trinity that we enjoy. But he knew God had promised a Redeemer and whether he dies or lives he would see this Redeemer for himself. That is faith, and God will not disappoint such faith. Job will be resurrected and he with his own two eyes will behold the Redeemer, Israel's Messiah, for himself.

Christ Returns Visibly

The Word of God makes it clear that that the return of the Christ to earth will be a globally visible event. Not just the event of descending to earth will be visible but His stay, reign, and activities. That truth is stated or implied in just about every scripture passage related to the second coming of the Christ in both testaments. Of course, the Old Testament only speak of the coming of the Lord or some equivalent term (e.g., Isa.63:1-6; Joel 3; Zech.14). Few passages are cited from the NT to make the case.

First, the passages where Jesus speaks of His return show that it will be personal and visible (John 14:1-3, 28). Saint Matthew records Jesus saying these words, "Immediately after the distress of those days the sun will be darkened, and the moon will not give its light; the stars will fall from the sky, and the heavenly bodies will be shaken. Then will appear the sign of the Son of Man in heaven. And then all the peoples of the earth will mourn when they see the Son of Man on the clouds of heaven, with power and great glory" (Matt.24:29-30). His visible personal presence will execute judgments upon His enemies (Matt.25:31-46).

Second, angels confirm that the return of the Christ will be a visible event. The utterance of the angels to those watching the Christ ascended into the heaven was, "Men of Galilee...why do you stand here looking into the sky? This same Jesus, who has been taken from you into heaven, will come back in the same way you have seen him go into heaven" (Acts 1:11).

Third, the apostles constantly preached, taught, and corrected false notions concerning the return of the Christ; to them the Lord's return will be personal and visible. Paul writes, "For the Lord Himself shall descend from heaven..." (1Thess.4:16). The apostle John gives us this intelligence report, "Look, he is coming with the clouds, and every eye will see him, even those who pierced him; and all peoples on earth will mourn because of him..." (Rev.1:7).

Christ Returns Publicly and Noisily

Christ will return publicly with shouts of triumph (1Thess.4:16). His ascension to heaven completes His first advent, and it was a public event of 120 witnesses, at least (Acts 1:15). Angels that watched Him depart in glory, reminded the human onlookers that "this same Jesus will come again in the manner they now see Him leave (Acts1:9-11). This is a clear indication that the Lord's return will be a visible, public event. Frankly, with the advent of mass media, His return will be viewed worldwide. The apostle John asserts that every eye shall behold Him upon His return (Rev.1:7). This is affirmation that the return of the Christ will be a widely public appearance. He is coming to judge all, no exemptions.

Jesus may have left for heaven without trumpet blast and shouting to attract the general public, but He is surely not coming back quietly. There will be shouting and trumpet blasting; the whole world will be looking up before they all drop to their knees. The Bible tells us that "the Lord himself shall descend from heaven with a shout, with the voice the archangel. And with the [trumpet] of God... (1Thess.4:16 KJV).

Christ Returns in Power and Glory

The person of the Christ is vested with the unimaginable power and glory of God; all God's fullness dwells in the Son (Col.1:19). When Bible scholars speak of such power, they use words like almighty, and omnipotent. There is no power in the universe that is equal to the power of God and His Christ. He speaks and planets are created; He speaks again, and they cease to exist.

Glory is the cumulative honors, splendor, royal possessions that constitute Majesty, all that makes a queen or king great. When the Queen of Sheba saw the glory of King Solomon, she fainted. She said, the half had never been told to her (1Kings 10:1-7). She was witnessing the sum of Solomon's glory, the sum of his greatness.

In the case of the Christ, glory includes a weighty presence with splendor brighter than the midday sun. The divine glory forces humans to the ground because there is a weightiness to it (Rev.1:12-18). Perhaps, it is this overwhelming, weighty presence, and brightness that force all knees to bow and all tongues to confess the Lordship of the Christ (Philip.2:9-11; Rev.5: 5-10). Moses was in the presence of God's glory forty days, and the glory transformed him. When he returned to his own people, they could not look upon him because of his dazzling facial radiance; he had to vail his face (Exod.35:27-33). "God is light" (1John1:5).

To become incarnate, the second person of the blessed Holy Trinity divested Himself of His majesty and glory and suspended the exercise of certain non-communicable attributes, such as omnipotence, omnipresence, and omniscience (Philip.2:5-8; John 1:1-2,14). A brief manifestation of this weighty splendor and glory, knocked three disciples off their feet when Jesus was transfigured before them on a mountain; they fell to the ground like dead men (Matt.17: 1-8)

These mighty powers and glory that were divested to become incarnate, were fully restored sometime after His resurrection or ascension. Christ is now majestically exalted to the highest place of power, authority, and glory (Philip.2: 8-11). The writer of the book of Hebrews speaks of this exalted position of the Christ when he said, "The Son is the radiance of God's glory and the exact representation of his being, sustaining all things by his powerful word..." (Heb.1: 3).

Furthermore, Jesus did pray to His Father for the restoration of the glory He divested Himself of to become incarnate (John 17:1-5). And we know that prayer was honored because Stephen saw the Christ after His ascension, at the Father's right hand in glory; the apostle John also saw Him fully vested in His glory restored and also fell to the ground (Acts 7: 55-60; Rev.1:9-20).

People who were not born in or lived in a kingdom vested Royal Majesty may find it hard envision the glory, pomp, and pageantry of a royal ascension. As I write this, I am watching with awe the investiture of Prince Charles as he assumes the position of King Charles III of the United Kingdom, guided by the Privy Council. Charles became King upon the death of his mother Queen Elizabeth II who reigned for 70 years.

The combined power and glory Queen Elizabeth II and King Charles III is trivial in the face of the reign, majesty, power, and glory of the Christ. Frankly, there is no comparison! It is therefore fitting that the Christ would return to earth in "power and great glory" (Matt.24:30; 25:31). "His glory is the manifestation" of "His visible splendor" as well as "His divine attributes and perfection."[1]

Christ Returns Suddenly and Dramatically

The return of the Christ to earth will be sudden, lightning fast. Jesus made it clear, "For as lightening that comes from the east is visible even in the west, so will be the coming of the Son of Man" (Matt.24:27). What is this verse telling us?

It is saying, because light travels at such a rapid speed, the lightening that flashes in the east instantly appears in the west as though it flashes in both places at once. This means there will be no time to get out of its path. There will be no time to prepare once the trumpet of Christ's return is blown. There will not be enough time to say, *"Lord have mercy,"* as the thief on the cross.

Despite the many signs notifying humankind of the near and pending return of the Christ, most unbelievers will not pay attention; it will take them unawares, like sudden disaster (1Thess.5:1-3). The world will be two busy making money and pleasure seeking. They will feel the birth pangs but ignore them.

Jesus sees a comparison with the unbelievers at His coming and the unbelievers before the great flood. Noah was a preacher of righteousness who warned his people a long time concerning the disaster that was coming. They ignored the warning and vilified the messenger, so despite Noah's preaching not one soul outside his family was saved. They all perished! (Gen.7:11-24).

Jesus predicts a similar happening at the time of His coming. The gospel message has been preached for two thousand years now, endeavoring to get people into the ark of safety, but billions ignore the massage of salvation and will perish (John 3:16). Jesus Himself gives us the following warning:

> As it was in the days of Noah, so it will be at coming of the Son of Man. For in the days before the flood, people were eating and drinking, marrying, and giving in marriage, up to the day Noah entered the ark; and they knew nothing about what would happen until the flood came and took them all away. That is how it will be at the coming of the Son of Man. (Matt.24:37-39)

The return of the Christs to earth will not only be sudden; it will be dramatic. Two Scripture passages capture this drama like none other. The first pictures the Christ leaving the portals of heaven on a milk whit stallion with armies of saints and angels. Here is the apostle John's depiction of the scene:

> I saw heaven standing open and there before mw was a white horse, whose rider is called Faithful and True. With justice he judges and wages war. His eyes are like blazing fire, and on his head are many crowns. He has a name written on him that no one knowns but he himself. He is dressed in a robe dipped in blood, and his name is the Word of God. The armies of heaven were following him, riding on white horses and dressed in fine linen, white and clean. Coming out of his mouth is a sharp sword with which to strike down the nations. He will rule them with an iron scepter. He treads the winepress of the fury of the wrath of God Almighty. On his robe and on his thigh, he has this name: KING OF KINGS AND LORD OF LORDS. (Rev.19:11-16)

The preceding Scripture passage needs no commentary; it speaks for itself with vivid clarity and eloquence. It broadcasts the status, rank, and purpose of this Commander in Chief leading His army to war. This is the Second Coming of the Christ, and it bears a striking contrast to His first coming as a baby in a manger. A baby poses no threat to anyone except the paranoid king Herod (Matt.2:1-23). This time Jesus comes as a conquering warrior and earth is prepared to repel Him as if He is an army of invading aliens.

There will be a coalition of nuclear armed nations under the leadership of the Antichrist waiting to repel the Christ from returning to the earth He created and owned (Psalm 24:1; 95:1-7). But He will be more than ready for them (Isa.63:1-6).

The second passage of descriptive drama applicable to the second coming of the Christ is from the Old Testament Prophet, Zechariah (chapter 14). While the apostle John in the preceding passage shows Christ descending from heaven in glory to earth, Zechariah depicts Him touching down on earth, standing on the Mount of Olives east of Jerusalem, where a coalition of nations under the Antichrist is already gathered to exterminate Israel. But the Christ arrives in the nick of time to abort the purpose of the wicked one and annihilation his armies instead.

Zechariah sees this as a unique day of judgment in all of history; he writes, on that day there will be neither sunlight nor cold, frosty darkness. It will be a unique day—a day known only to the LORD—with no distinction between day and night. When evening comes, there will be light" (v.6).

But first the prophet gives this descriptive phenomenon: "On that day his feet will stand on the Mount of Olives, east of Jerusalem, and the Mount of Olives will be split in two from east to west, forming a great valley, with half of the mountain moving north and half moving south" (v.4). The return of the Christ is indeed dramatic, and this is just the beginning of His reign.

Christ Returns with Company

Christ will not return to earth alone but with a great company of saints and angels referred to as the armies of heaven (Col.3:1-4; Jude 14-15; Rev.19:11-21). Frankly, His ascension to heaven was not alone, in as much as Luke does not record Him leaving with any company (Acts 1:9-11). There are two schools of thought concerning this issue; we will briefly explore them.

First, that Christ came out of the tomb on resurrection morning with a great hosts of Old Testament saints. Because the three days He was out of the body He was in Paradise, a place believed to be somewhere in the underworld. Jesus told the repentant thief on the cross, "Truly I tell you, today you will be with me in Paradise" (Luke 23 39-43). Paradise is used in connection with the garden of Eden, also a place where the righteous would go in the afterlife. It is said to be a Persian word, meaning a park or pleasure garden, a place of bliss.[2] What is important is that Jesus said he was going there with the converted thief that very day, and they could not be going there in the physical body. Christ's confirmation is strong and indisputable.

Jesus Himself gives us added insight into this underworld place in a story about a rich, uncompassionate man who died and was buried, and a poor righteous man named, Lazarus, who died and was taken to Paradise (a/k/a Abraham's bosom). Both men showed up in the underworld, but in different compartments. One in a place of torment, the other in Paradise, a place of comfort. They could not cross over to each other or comeback to this life at will but they were alive and conscious (Luke 16:19-31).

The apostle Peter also speaks of this underworld place that Jesus went the three days He was out of the body. Peter asserts:

> For Christ also suffered once for sins, the just for the unjust, that He might bring us to God, being put to death in the flesh but made alive in the Spirit, by whom also He went and preach to the spirits in prison, who formerly were disobedient, when once the Divine longsuffering waited in the days of Noah, while the ark was being prepared, in which a few, that is, eight souls, were saved through water. (1Peter 3:18-20 NKJV)

The preceding quote from Peter is viewed by scholars as controversial, and there is no unanimous agreement as to what it means. In the light of other passages, some scholars believe that Jesus indeed went into the underworld to preach to those souls. Others say, "the spirits are the souls of people who died in the great flood of Noah" indeed (Gen.6-7). But "the preaching was done by the pre-incarnate Christ through Noah's preaching to his disobedient contemporaries...."[3] For this author, this second view seems farfetched. The apostle Paul gives us this intelligence report:

> But to each one of us grace has been given as Christ apportioned it. This is why it says: 'When he ascended on high, he took many captives and gave gifts to his people.' (What does he ascended mean except that he also descended to the lower earthly regions? He who descended is the very one who ascended higher than the heavens, in order to fill the whole universe). So Christ himself gave the apostles, the prophets, the evangelist, the pastors and teachers, to equip his people for works of service.... (Eph.4. 7-12)

Scholars explain the preceding quote to mean that the resurrected, ascended, exalted Christ distributes gifts to His Church as a King in ancient times returning from war divides the spoils with his troops. The "descended to the lower earthly regions" is no more than Christ coming to the earth from heaven as the incarnate Son of God. This limited explanation does not settle the matter for me.

When the passage is paraphrased and summarized, such explanation seems plausible. But when examined word for word and in the light of other passages, such limited explanation seems troubling. There is a bias against the notion that while Christ was out of the body He went to Paradise as He said to the dying thief.

The Spirit of Christ must have been somewhere the three days while His body was in the grave. That somewhere must have been the underworld where Paradise was said to be.

Second, if Christ led captivity captive when He ascended on high, then He did not return to heaven alone and that warrants explanation. One explanation is when he descended in the underworld, He transferred Paradise from down to up. In his classic hymn, *Christ the Lord is Risen Today,* Charles Wesley penned these words insightful words:

> Love's redeeming work is done, Allelula!
> Fought the fight, the battle won, Allelula!
> Death in vain forbids Him rise, Allelula!
> Christ has opened Paradise, Allelula!

Christ told the repentant thief on the cross, today you will be with me in Paradise. Matthew gives us this intelligence report:

> And Jesus cried out again with a loud voice and yielded up His spirit. Then, behold, the veil of the temple was torn in two from top to bottom; and the earth quaked, and the rocks were split, and the graves were opened; and many bodies of the saints who had fallen asleep were raised, and coming out of the graves after His resurrection, they went into the holy city and appeared to many. (Matt.27:49-52)

Now, if a multitude of Old Testament saints came out of their graves at the time of Christ's resurrection, then that would be consistent with the view that Christ went to Paradise and by extension transferred Paradise to an upward or heavenly location.

We are only left with one question to answer, when did He ascend with these saints to the upward Paradise? This question lends itself to two possible answers: 1) immediately after the resurrection before He met with His disciples, or 2) at the ascension forty days later.

While it is logical to assert that immediately after His resurrection, our Lord made a quick trip to heaven to report to His Father and escort those saints to their relocated Paradise, then returned to earth to debrief His disciples for the next forty-days, we have no scriptural support for such theory. We must consider that explanation possible but a fanciful stretch.

The more plausible position would be that these saints were caught up with Christ at the time of His ascension. They were not seen because they were not occupying a resurrection body like our Lord's body; they were disembodied spirits, and therefore seen by no one else. Jesus Christ is the firstfruits of them that slept. The true resurrection for these saints is still in the future. *Their status has not changed only their location.* It is like transferring a sleeping person from one room to another.

While this discussion does not answer all the question, we must leave it here for now. Other scripture passages quoted earlier tell us Jesus did not ascend alone, and we are sure he is not returning to earth alone. He will be accompanied with an army of saints and angels (1Thess.4:16; Jude 14-15; Rev.19:11-14).

CHAPTER 5

HOW WILL CHRIST BE RECEIVED UPON HIS RETURN?

With the gospel finally reached all the nations of the world, and humankind experienced the apocalyptic hand of divine judgment in the *Great Tribulation* and the failure of government without God to alleviate their problems, one would have thought the world would be ready to welcome the Lord Jesus Christ on bended knees; that they would be waving palm branches to welcome Him as creator and rightful owner of this earth.

But that will not be the case, I can assure you! While some humans will be glad to see the KING of Kings and LORD of Lords, the vast majority of persons will certainly not happy to see Him.

They will not welcome His arrival. To them, Christ has come to disrupt their party and sit in judgment against them. For that they are hostile, gnashing their teeth in hate against Him.

Perhaps, the march into Jerusalem on His first advent, during the week of His passion, holds clues to the reception Christ will receive on His second advent. His entrance into the city on that first Palm Sunday was greeted with a jubilant, cheering crowd, shouting, "Hosanna to the Son of David!" "Blessed is he who comes in the name of the Lord!" "Hosanna in the highest heaven!" (Matt. 21:9). But few days later, the lyrics of their chant changed to "Crucify Him! Crucify!" (Matt.27: 22-23).

The hostile crowd then was led by Caiaphas, the high priest; he convinced the Roman governor to execute Jesus, despite being declared innocent on all charges. This condemnation did not take Jesus by surprise; He forecasted this murderous treatment in the parable of the *Wicked Vinedressers (Matt.21:33-39)*.

The parable asserts that that there was a certain landowner who planted a vineyard and set a hedge around it, dug a winepress in it and build a tower. And he leased it to vinedressers and went into a far country. When vintage time drew near; he sent his servants to the vinedressers to collect his share. But vinedressers caught the servants, beat one, killed the one, and stoned another.

Again, other servants were sent, and they received the same cruel treatment. Finally, the vineyard owner sent his son, believing they would respect his son. But when they saw him, they said among themselves. This is the heir. Come, let us kill him and seize his inheritance. So they took him and cast him out of the vineyard and killed him (Matt.21:33-39 NKJV).

Jesus concluded the parable by asking His listeners this question, "Therefore, when the owner of the vineyard comes, what will he do with those vinedressers?" (v.40). They replied, "He will destroy those wicked men miserably, and lease his vineyard to other vinedressers who will render to him the fruits in their season" (v.41). The religious elite audience, not knowing that they are the vinedressers implicated in the parable, condemned themselves.

To drive home the application of the parable, Jesus went on to say to them, "Have you never read in the Scriptures: 'The stone which the builders rejected Has become the chief cornerstone. This was the Lord's doing, and it is marvelous in our eyes?'"

The rejected stone in the quote is Jesus Himself, and the builders who rejected Him are the religious leaders of Israel to who he was speaking. They are the vinedressers who killed God's prophets that were sent to them, and they are the ones now positioning themselves to kill the Son of God, which they later did by crucifixion. Based on their rejection of Him, Jesus pronounced judgment upon Israel's religious leaders. Of course, they had already pronounced judgment upon themselves.

Note the judgment Jesus pronounced upon them--"Therefore, I say to you, the kingdom of God will be taken from you and given to a nation bearing the fruits of it. And whoever falls on this stone will be broken, but on whomever it falls, it will grind him to powder" (Matt.21:43-44).

The Christian Church represents God's kingdom upon the earth; it is God's holy nation (1Peter 2:9-10). It is comprised of Jews and gentiles, but largely gentile nations because Israel as a nation rejected Jesus as their Messiah. For this reason, they will accept an imposter, the Antichrist as their messiah (2 Thess.2: 9-12). But the

Antichrist is a wolf in sheep clothing; he will later turn and devour them as wolf devours sheep.

On His second advent, Jesus returns to rescue Israel in the nick of time from annihilation by gentile nations who also rejected Him. This time around, it will not be Caiaphas, Pilate or Caesar in charge, but Jesus Christ Himself as KING of Kings LORD of Lords.

A Hostile Reception

Christ and His people will first and foremost face a hostile reception upon their arrival on earth. The welcoming committee will be a coalition of nuclear armed nations with all the firepower earth has stock pilled over the decades.

These weapons of mass destruction will be under the commanded of the Antichrist and the False prophet who are the human agents of Satan and his One-world government. These two beast-men will have all the powers and wizardry of Satan (Rev.13: 1-18). Satan will imitate the Holy Trinity but there will be nothing holy about him or anyone in his circle of influence.

For seven years this unholy trinity (Satan, the Antichrist, the False prophet) have controlled all of life: the economic system, commerce, business, law, government, education, travel, agriculture, labor, technology, worship, health, everything.

But the fundamental thing Satan wants is worship, and that is what he wants above all else, worship. And for seven years the whole world will worship him, many voluntarily, but others by force. Those who refused to worship him, he will destroy. There will be pockets of resistance in every country, but in due season secret police will flush them out and stamp out.

One priority is to get rid of Israel, the nation that stubbornly refused to bend the knees before the Antichrist. Israel is marked for annihilation. Her annihilation will serve as an example to any other nation that wishes to oppose the one-world government.

The Antichrist has his sight fixed on Israel and vows to finish what Hitler did not finish and other devils were too timid to carryout. He invades and isolates Israel, besieges Jerusalem, and mercilessly tightens the noose to surrender that he can annihilate them. Israel has been in vulnerable places before, but nothing like this since Moses brought them out of Egyptian slavery.

From a political perspective, Israel is between a rock and a hard place because United States is no longer a world power to defend her. So, in return for economic and military security, Israel signs a treaty with the Antichrist's government for favored nation status, when he first emerged on the scene. But the Antichrist is a deceiver and has no intension of abiding by the treaty. Once the Antichrist consolidates his global power, he abandons the treaty with Israel.

The Antichrist is not the Messiah, he presents himself to be. He is the agent of Satan, almost *diabolos* incarnate. Now Israel is forced to worship Satan through this beast-man, the ultimate idolatry forbidden by the Torah. Israel must now face extinction because there is no nation on earth that can come her defense. But before the military machine of the Antichrist completes the mission of extermination and annihilation of God's covenant people, there comes the disruption of divine intervention.

The Eastern sky split asunder by the majestic form of the returning Christ; He is accompanied by a massive army of saints and angels. He is riding a milk white stallion and rapidly descending and advancing toward Jerusalem. His face shines above the intensity of the midday sun, and all the armies of earth are forced to their knees. The battlelines are drawn and the countdown to the final war has begun (for details, see Volume 6, Armageddon).

A Colossal Military Miscalculation

The Antichrist military planners made more than a miscalculation to invade Israel and besieged Jerusalem to annihilate them. They made a fatal, colossal miscalculation. They thought no nation on earth was left with the military power to stand with Israel to defend themselves. They were right but still wrong; this was a divine set up to get these wicked nations in one place for God to judge and destroy them.

In fact, it was God's doing. But they had no idea it was God bringing them into that part of the world to execute judgment on them. They thought they were doing it at their own accord, that they chose the time and place for Israel's destruction, but instead, God compelled them to gather for their own destruction.

This is what God says through the prophet Zechariah, "I will gather all nations to Jerusalem to fight against it….Then the Lord will go out and fight against those nations... (Zech.14:2-3).

The prophet Joel also speaks to this gathering of nations against Israel as God's doing. "I will gather all nations and bring them down to the valley of Jehoshaphat. There I will put them on trial for what they did to my inheritance, my people Israel, because they scattered my people among the nations and divided up my land. They cast lots for my people and traded boys for prostitutes; they sold girls for wine to drink" (Joel 3:2-3).

Upon His return, Jesus will sit as judge over the nations as Zechariah, Joel, Isaiah, and Ezekiel prophesied. Jesus Himself gives us this intelligence report, "When the Son of Man comes in his glory and all the angels with him, he will sit on his glorious throne. All nations will be gathered before him, and he will separate the people one from another as a shepherd separates the sheep from the goats" (Matt.25:31-32).

The administration of justice will be in the hands of the Christ no sooner than He arrives upon earth at His second advent. Nations are made accountable for their atrocities, especially those gathered in the *Middle East* to destroy God's covenant people, Israel. God made this promise to Abraham, "I will make you a great nation, and I will bless you; …. I will bless those who bless you, and whoever curses you I will curse and all peoples on the earth will be blessed through you" (Gen.12 1-3). Perhaps America's blessing is tied to her commitment to stand with Israel.

It is evident from the promise that to fight the people of God is to fight God. The is also evident in the conversion of Saul of Tarsus who set himself to destroy the infant Church. The risen Lord and Christ who struck him down from his horse and said to him, "Saul, Saul, why are you persecuting me?" (Acts 9:1-5). Hitler and all who stood with him will face judgment by Jesus Christ.

The Final War

Jesus returns to earth as the General who commands the armies of heaven (Rev.19:11-21). This is undoubtedly an army of saints and angels. This is no ordinary army; they are superior in number, power, and glory. Humans are in their glorified body and already overcome death; they die no more. The saints are innumerable (Rev.7:9-) but they will not be engaged in fighting.

The angels with Christ are also innumerable and of various strength and levels of authority (Heb.12:22 KJV). In as much as one angel killed 185,000 Assyrian troops in one night (2 Kings 19:35); there is no evidence they will be fighting upon Christ return. It appears as if Christ Himself will do all the fighting (Rev.19:11-15). And it will not be for the want of firepower.

Upon arrival, Jesus will encounter the collective and hostile armed forces of earth positioned for war. He strikes them down with the sword of His mouth (i.e., His word). Scholars refer to this war as Armageddon; it is the war that ends all wars. Jesus will suffer no casualties in His army. But millions of troops and commanders of various ranks from earths armies will be dead when the dust clears. Birds of prey will be called to assist in the clean up by devouring much flesh (Rev.19: 17-18, 21).

A trial is held often referred to by scholars as the Judgment of Nations. Some nations are destroyed, while others are allowed to enter with Christ in His millennial reign (Matt.25:31-46).

In as much as Christ purposefully returns in the nick of time to save Israel from annihilation, they also will be judged for their treatment and rejection of the Messiah (Rev.20:4-5). But God has reserved a remnant that will be saved. At this time all Israel will embrace Jesus as their Messiah and all that do so will be saved and enter with Him in His millennial kingdom (Rom.11:1-32).

Summary

The Lord Jesus Christ upon His return will not be greeted and welcome by friendly humans. The people who are friends of Christ are returning with Him. Most of the people on earth at the time of His coming are antichrist's people, enemies of Christ. But most of them will be civilians and will not be in the Middle East at the scene of the war to directly engage Christ in combat.

The fighters are military personnel, those in the armed forces are loyalists of the antichrist, enemies of the Christ. They are tasked to fight any authority opposed to the antichrist system of government. These fighters and support personnel will be in the millions and will be slain at Christ command. Birds of prey will be summoned to assist in the cleanup of the slain (Rev.20:19-21).

Jesus will touchdown in a war zone and immediately faced with the collective hostile armed forces of earth. They will have all the technological gismos of modern warfare at their disposal, including the combined nuclear arsenal of earth at their command. No ordinary army can match the firepower they have at their command. Yet despite all that military capability, they will be no match for the Lord Jesus Christ. The one who is infinite, omnipotent, and Almighty. Isaiah 63 depicts what will happen; he will trample them as one tramples grapes in a winepress.

This will be the final war waged against evil but not the final battle; there will be a few more battles or skirmishes that will be easily put down by the Lord Jesus. There is no power or authority that the Christ is subservient to—since His resurrection, all authority has been given in heaven and earth (Matt.28:18).

Satan is in prison for a thousand years, and during this time, the earth will enjoy peace and prosperity. Some evil will still be around but not with the prior intensity because Satan is in prison, and Jesus is King ruling over the earth.

At the end of the thousand years or millennium, Satan will be paroled for a short time to take care of business; that gives him time to lead one last rebellion against Christ and His people.

But fire comes down out of heaven and consumed Satan's human followers; Satan himself is permanently cast into hell to join the beast (the antichrist) and the false prophet (Rev.20:7-12).

The next big event is the Final Judgment, also called the White Throne judgment. The wicked dead of all ages will come back to life to be judged and thrown into hell with Satan, the god whom they served (Rev.20:11-15). See volumes 9 and 10.

The people of God have a bright future that is eternal. We have every reason to live in faith and home because He who promised is faithful. The pilgrimage is at time dark and trying but like Jesus who endured the cross, despising its shame and is now seated at the right hand of the Majesty on high we must endure likewise for the rewards are great.

CHAPTER 6

YOUR ATTITUDE TOWARD THE COMING OF THE CHRIST

This closing chapter speaks to three readership audiences: the Christian, the seeker, and the unbeliever.

The Christian audience is consisted of different groups of people who practice the faith to one degree or another, and believe they possess eternal life and are on their way to heaven. The seekers are those people who want to believe but they have many questions that they want to get answered before they make a commitment to follow Christ.

The unbelievers are those who have no place for God and Christ in their life and thought. To them Christianity is irrelevant, fiction, and holds no promise. Yet, they are not quite comfortable with spending their eternity in the lake of burning sulfur, so they would not mind sharing destination with the Christian. Since everybody wants to end up in a happy place, I am volunteering to be the guide.

The Christian Audience

Wearing the lifestyle label, Christian, is no guarantee you are a child of God going to heaven. I do not mean to frighten you. But I hope it causes you to sit-up straight, because I want you to be fully awake to hear some sobering things many believers are trying to ignore detriment. Rather than ignoring it, its best we face the critique, and go through the process of self-examination now. Don't wait like the five foolish virgins that got locked out (Matt. 25:1-13).

Had they done self-check, they would have discovered their lack of readiness and remedy the situation in time. And how different the story would have been! We would have ten wise virgins and no foolish ones. The word of God exhorts us to be wise, wise as serpents, and if you lack wisdom ask of God (James 1:5).

God wants people with insight and foresight, not just hindsight. He wants people who have all contingencies covered because that is the time you are truly ready. Before a jet takes off, the pilots carefully go through a checklist of critical things that could put that jet in crisis mode at 35 thousand feet in the air. The word of God calls the believer to take inventory from time to time. Why is self-check necessary? The short answer is that people tend to be careless, and careless about important things.

Here is the uncomfortable truth many Christians don't want to admit or face. You can be baptized in water, attend church regularly, and even participate in its ministries of teaching, preaching, leading, charity giving and the like, and still miss heaven. How do I know this? Here what Jesus Himself said, "Not everyone who says to me, Lord, Lord, will enter the kingdom of heaven." He goes on to say, "Many will say to me on that day, Lord, Lord, did we not prophesy in your name and in your name drive out demons and, in your name, perform many miracles? Then I will tell them plainly, I never knew you. Away from me, you evildoers!" (Matt. 7: 21-23). Let us reflect on the quote a little bit. You will see why it frightens me.

These are the reasons it frightens me: (1) The person speaking. This is Jesus talking. The kingdom is His and He does not make idle talk. He knows what is in all of us, and He determines who gets in and who does not cut the proverbial mustard to get in.

(2) He is talking about that day, the Day of Judgment. There is no time to correct anything, no second chance, no clean this up and come back in two weeks. It is eternally over!

(3) The people that He does not know, have been in ministry for a long time, and they had good success. They prophesied (preach), teach, cast out demons, did healing miracles, and other miracles. They were baptized in water and connected to a local church.

(4) In my name. They got results using the name of Jesus, and it gave them a false sense of security that they were okay for heaven, but in reality, they were not.

If Jesus does not know you, it means, you do not know Him even though you make think you do. Make sure the relationship is reciprocal; you know Him, and He knows you. The following guiding principles are guardrails to keeps us in a state of productive readiness waiting for the second coming of the Christ.

- *Examine yourself your connection to Jesus Christ.* Paul exhorts the Corinthians to examine their faith, to test themselves to determine if they are in the faith or not (2

Cor.13: 51). He used the same language of self-examination when these same folks were guilty of abusing the Lord's Supper (1Cor.11:28). See if you are truly born again according to the word of God (John 3:1-5, 16). Have you turned away from the sinful lifestyle through a personal encounter with Jesus Christ that has transformed your life? (Rom. 12:1-3).

- *Ensure your life been led by the blessed Holy Spirit.* You are still governed by your carnal nature, and there is hardly any change has taken place in your life (Rom.8:5-10).

- *Don't waste your time, live a productive for Christ.* True Christian life produces the fruit of the Spirit, the Holy Spirit (Gal.5:22-23). There are nine graces in this portion of Scripture that are produced by the Holy Spirit in the believer's life. The believer also has a responsibility to help cultivate the fruit of the Spirit by abiding in Christ and cooperating with Him (John 15:1-8).

- *We make the business of Christ kingdom our priority.* Jesus said, seek first the kingdom of heaven and his righteousness (Matt.6:33). Such people tend not to serve the unrighteous mammon, have divided spirit loyalty, or store up treasures on earth. They live useful, productive lives here while keeping an eye on eternity. They story of the rich fool points us in the right direction (Luke 12:16-21).The man in this story is not called a fool because he was successful and rich. He is labeled a fool because he lays up treasures on earth but none in heaven (v.21). He was rich in material things, but poor in the spiritual life.

- *We serve Christ out of love and obedience.* Love is the identifying mark of a true child of God (1John 3:10-23). John knows this because Jesus said it. "By this shall all persons know that you are my disciples if you have love one for another." Love is the new commandment (John 13:34-35). Genuine Christian love is reflected in our obedience to Christ. "If you love me, keep my commandment" of love and obedience (John 15:10-17).

- *Finally, we serve God by serving people.* That was the example Jesus set with His own life; He served others out of love. He declares, "whoever wants to be great among you must be the servant of all. For even the Son of Man did not come to be served but to serve and to give His life a ransom for many (Matt.20:28). When we serve others in love, we secure a reward in God's kingdom. On that day of judgment, the King of the kingdom will say to those who serve in love, "inasmuch as you have done it to the least of these my brethren you have done it unto me" (Matt.25: 34-40).

The person that has truly experienced more than an encounter with Christ but whose life has transformed by His grace, and through love and obedience serve Christ and neighbor should hear well done good and faithful servant on that day of final reckoning. But until the trumpet sounds or we fall asleep in death, use the guideline points of this section to make periodic self-check to avoid being deception (Matt.24:4-5). The greatest deception of all is self-deception, so take nothing for granted (Gal.6:6-10).

To those who serve in places of leadership, a special warning. We who serve God's people in places of leadership, especially pastors, are held to a higher level of accountability by people and by Christ Himself. Coming to the end of His ministry on earth, Jesus accounted to the Father for the disciples entrusted to Him. In prayer to the Father He said, "I have revealed you to those whom you gave me out of the world.... None has been lost except the one doomed to destruction so that Scripture would be fulfilled" (John 17: 8-12).

The lesson here is that accountability is intrinsic to servant leadership. This is true not only in secular life but in the spiritual life as well, a concept frequently replicated in the gospels and throughout the rest of the NT. For example, Jesus speaks about the unjust steward (   ), the householder that gave a sum of money to three of his servants to invest before he went off on a long journey and later returned to reckon (   ), the parable of the rented winepress, and the parable of the barren fig tree. These stories are told illustrate that there is one to whom we are all accountable who judge us at some time in the future.

Jesus was particularly tough with the leaders of Judaism because they were the ones in charge of the spiritual life of his people Israel. They made it difficult for the people to serve God, putting heavy loads or requirements on them that they themselves did not do. The leaders of the new Israel of God, the Church, will be held to no less accountability. To this end, the author of the epistle to the Hebrews twice draws attention to those who lead God's people. First, "Remember your leaders, who spoke the word of God to you. Consider the outcome of their way of life and imitate their faith" (Heb.13:7). The congregation should hold them up as a pattern of example. A bad leader can lead the flock straight off the cliff.

Second, "Have confidence in your leaders and submit to their authority, because they keep watch over you as those who must give an account. Do this so that their work will be a joy not a burden, for that would be of no benefit to you" (v.17).

This second exhortation is a reminder to both shepherd and sheep that they have a responsibility to each other before God. The sheep should submit to the authority of the shepherd not making it difficult for the shepherd to lead. On the other hand, the shepherd must not abuse his authority of leadership because he must give account to the Chief Shepherd, Jesus Christ (1 Peter). Jesus will be no less tough on the leaders of the Christian flock than He was on the leaders of Judaism. So, those of us who are given the care of the flock of God must be particularly careful.

The Seekers' Audience

The seekers are those people with a keen interest in the spiritual life, but they have a thousand or more questions they want answered about God, the Bible, creation, where Cain got his wife, and many others before they commit themselves to Christ. Some in this group are sincere seekers, while others use it as an excuse to show off their knowledge.

The sincere seeker deserves answer to his or her questions. The Christian has a duty and an obligation to provide reasonable answers to questions about the faith. The apostle Peter exhorts believers to "be always ready to give a defense to everyone who asks you a reason for the hope that is in you, with meekness and fear…" (1Peter 3:15 NKJ). In this context, meekness and fear means, humility and respect.

The sincere seeker is intellectually honest and will submit to reasonable truth. When the disciple, Thomas, was told that Jesus is risen from the dead and seen by the others, he said he would not believe until shown evidence. He wanted to see the nail prints in Jesus' hands and his side where the sword pierced. When he encountered Jesus next, he was allowed to examine the evidence for himself. But Jesus gave him prior caution to believe upon the basis of the evidence. When Thomas saw the evidence, he fell to his knees and said, "My Lord and my God!" (John 20:28).

Thomas was a sincere seeker, so he submitted himself to the evidence. Not to surrender to the evidence would have brought him into the dangerous territory of unbelief. That was the reason for Jesus' prior caution to him. The insincere seeker will not submit to evidence because he does not really need an answer; he wants to parade his knowledge by perpetual questioning.

To the sincere seeker, I say, it's time to make your commitment to Jesus Christ, receive forgiveness of sin, and the gift of eternal life (John 3:16). Christianity has amassed over two thousand years of evidence to answer all your sincere questions about the faith. It is time to commit. Jesus knowing that not everyone will have the opportunity to personally examine his hands and side said to Thomas, "Blessed are they that have not seen, yet believing" (20:29).

Christianity is a life of faith, no one is going to get all questions answered before coming into a personal relationship with Jesus, because the relationship is necessary to the understanding of some things. The Word of God clearly asserts that the natural person cannot understand the things of God for they are spiritually discerned. If you want to make heaven you must first have a saving relationship with Jesus Christ, and it begins with the step of faith.

The Audience of Unbelievers

My first word to the unbeliever is, God owes you nothing, absolutely nothing! Yet, He has given you everything to make your life comfortable on this earth with a few problems here and there. He Has given you the gift of life, health, family, sunlight, water, the ability to earn your keep, and many other gifts. Above all, He offers you the gift of eternal life through His Son Jesus Christ. It is a gift of His grace (John 3:16; Eph.2:8).

Salvation is free to us humans but not cheap; it cost God the life of His Son. You cannot get to heaven if you bypass Jesus Christ. It is an exercise in futility just to try; it will not happen! You are more likely to end up in a very uncomfortable place with very high temperature and for a very long time (John 3:16). Smart people accept the offer of salvation, but fools ignore it like the man in the story of the rich fool (Luke 12:13-21).

My final word to the unbeliever is this, "...unless you repent, you will all likewise perish (Luke 13:1-5). It seems harsh but it is the loving truth. A change of lifestyle is what Jesus demands and you cannot bring about that radical change by yourself, you must come to the Lord for His help (Luke 24:46-47; Acts 2:36-39).

The Morally Good Person

The morally good person is in a category of unbelievers who believe the existence of God, heaven, and hell. But he cherishes the false notion that there are many roads that lead to eternal life and heaven, that there is more than one holy book to be used as guide.

So, there is no need binding yourself just to the Bible or Jesus, that he is just as good as them Christians.

Yes, by human's standard, there are many morally good people in this world, but by God's standard, there are no good people. The Word of God states, "There is none righteous, no not one" (Rom.9-18 KJV). The Bible further declares, "For all have sinned and come short of the glory of God" (v. 23).

The morally good person says, there are many roads to eternal life and heaven, but that is false, such beliefs lead straight to hell. If anyone knows about eternal life and heaven Jesus should know because He is the giver of eternal life, and He came from heaven and returned to heaven and is coming again (John 3:16; Acts 1:9-11). This is what Jesus said, "Enter by the narrow gate; for wide is the gate and broad is the way that leads to destruction, and there are many who go into it. Because narrow is the way which leads to life, and there are few who find it" (Matt.7:13-14).

On this question of eternal life and heaven, the Lord Jesus Christ is the final authority. The broad road with many lanes does not lead to eternal life or heaven, it leads to destruction or hell. The way to heaven is a singular road with a narrow gate and the gate and way is Jesus Christ (John 14:1-6).

Good works is a poor substitute for salvation from sin, if you have eternal life and heaven on your mind; good work will not suffice. Salvation is God's gift of grace to you; you can never work for it (Eph.2: 8-9). After you receive this free gift of God's grace in Jesus Christ, God will accept your good works offered to Him in love (v.10). You cannot contribute anything to the provision of your salvation but to repent of your sins and receive God's gift. Think of eternal life and heaven as whole life salvation policy with premium full paid. All you must do is to take the policy home; its free to you, though costing God the life of His Son (John 3:16-17).

Summary

As we wait for the glorious return of the Christ, the believers are encouraged to be in a constant state of readiness and watchfulness because for us, the rapture is really what we are waiting for. But we do not sit around passively or idly waiting; we continue to serve Christ and neighbors in love. We do self-check to ensure we are truly connected to Christ; we are not among the self-deceived ones.

Those who are seekers are encouraged not only to look to the witnessing believer to get your questions answered but do your own research. There is over two thousand years of historical evidence Christianity has amassed. Lee Strobel, once and atheist when researching to disprove Christianity but ended up being convinced by the evidence he uncovered. Strobel became an apologist in defense of the faith. He wrote the book, *Evidence that Demands a Verdict*.

It is time for the seeker to make his or her commitment to Jesus Christ for time is running out.

The unbeliever is prodded to repent or run the risk of perishing (John 3:16). The destination of the unbeliever is the lake of burning sulfur and every day he moves closer to that hellish destination. Jesus tells us the unbeliever is already condemned (John 3:18-21). So, this is no time for quiet, politically correct talk while millions, if not billions, slide to that place where the fire is not quenched and the worms die not, that place where "there will be weeping and gnashing of teeth" (Luke 13:28). We can help but shout, repent! It is the loving thing to do. My hope and prayer that the seeker comes to the right decision about Jesus in a timely manner.

END NOTES

Chapter 1

1. The relationship between the Christianity and secular (Rome) was a volatile and adversarial until Constantine who paved the way for the Church to take the seat of power. That relationship is captured in Kenneth R. Himes' landmark work, *Christianity and the Political Order: Conflict, Cooptation, and Cooperation*. Maryknoll, New York: Orbis Books, 2013.

Chapter 2

1. Christ will return to judge the living and the dead is doctrinal statement of the Church from that the apostolic era that is reflected in Church's creed from the earliest of times and remains constant. The main creeds and how they come about are reflected in a book by Justin S. Holcomb, *Know the Creeds and Councils*. Grand Rapids, MI: Zondervan, 2014.

Chapter 3

1. Certain details on the temple built by Herod the Great as a gift to the Jewish people are reflected in the Holman Study Bible, NKJV Edition footnote on Luke 21:5 (p.1756).

2. Ibid.

Chapter 4

1. On the "Day of the Lord" and the "Day of Christ" see entry in Merrill F. Unger, R.K. Harrison, Editor, *The New Unger's Bible Dictionary*. Chicago: Moody Bible Institute, 1988 (286).

2. Ibid, 287.

3. Holman Study Bible, NKJV, 2118

Chapter 5

1. The New Unger's Bible Dictionary, *Glory*, 479

2. Ibid, *Paradise*, 962.

ABOUT THE AUTHOR

Michael W. Dewar, Sr. is a pastor, Bible teacher, and mentor in the spiritual life. He is a Licensed Master Social Worker, and a specialist in church and family conflicts. He trains Agents of Peace-Managers of Conflicts to launch peace ministries in local churches.

Reverend Dewar is the founder and pastor of New York Congregational Baptist Church (NYCBC), and the author of several books, including a three-volume training course on Church and Family Conflicts.

He holds earned degrees from several institutions of higher learning, including the Master of Divinity from what is now Palmer Theological Seminary, Eastern University, the MSW from Wurzweiler School of Social Work, Yeshiva University, the LMSW from the State of New York, and the D.MIN from Regent University, School of Divinity.

Reverend Dewar lives in NYC with his family.

THE SECOND COMING OF THE CHRIST

OTHER BOOKS BY THIS AUTHOR

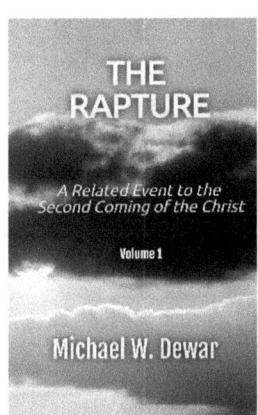

Volume 3

Second Edition   First Edition

Launch a peace ministry in your church using this textbook plus Instructor's Manual and Students' Manual (not shown here).

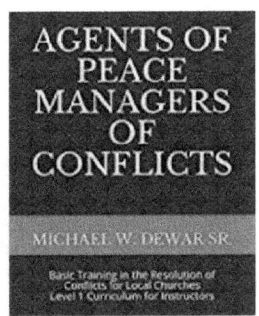 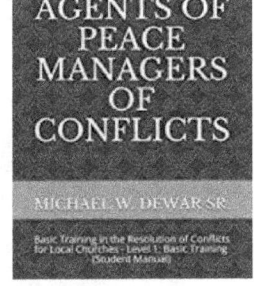

Instructor's Manual   **Students' Manual**

This is a course of study for launching a peace ministry in your church for the management and resolution of conflicts. Used with the textbook Church and Family Conflicts

Vol.1 The Rapture, **Vol.2** The Believers Judgment & Reward, **Vol.3** The Great Tribulation Survival Guide….

Volume 3

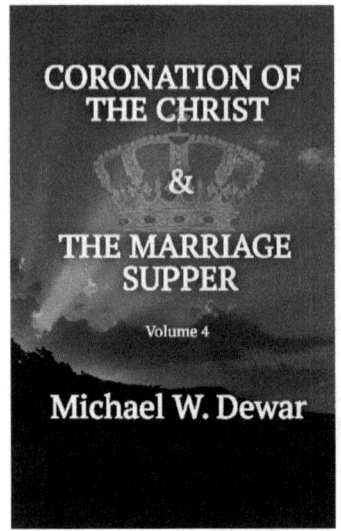 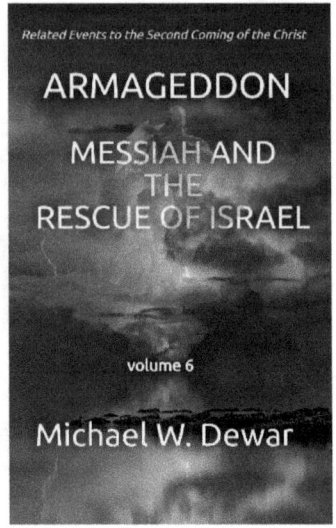

Feedback and support welcome at: DPSCLEANSING.COM

THE SECOND COMING OF THE CHRIST

www.ingramcontent.com/pod-product-compliance
Lightning Source LLC
Chambersburg PA
CBHW071723040426
42446CB00011B/2191